P9-CMS-730

SUCCESSFUL Wrestling

WM. C. BROWN COMPANY PUBLISHERS, Dubuque, Iowa

SUCCESSFUL
Wrestling

ITS BASES AND PROBLEMS

ARNOLD W. UMBACH, M.A.
Head Professor of Men's Physical Education
Westling Coach, Alabama Polytechnic Institute

and

WARREN R. JOHNSON, Ed.D.
Professor of Health and Physical Education
University of Maryland
formerly Varsity Wrestling Coach at
Boston University

WM. C. BROWN COMPANY PUBLISHERS, *Dubuque, Iowa*

Copyright, 1953, by the C. V. Mosby Company

Copyright, 1960
by
Arnold W. Umbach
and
Warren R. Johnson

Library of Congress Catalog Card Number: 60-13248

We have long felt that there is a definite need for a book on American amateur wrestling that goes beyond what has been written before. We joined forces to prepare this book for both the coaching and class teaching situations.

In addition to covering the subject of amateur wrestling as thoroughly as possible, *Successful Wrestling* offers the following special features:

1. Pictorial Analysis (Drawings) of Wrestling Maneuvers. The illustrative drawings are from championship movies and from still photographs. Every important step in each maneuver is clearly shown. There is no need to guess what happened between pictures. The defensive wrestler and the offensive wrestler are clearly delineated; there are none of the distracting shadows that are inevitable in photographic analysis. Descriptions and comments below the drawings stress the crucial points in the sequences.

Since several drawings were often required to clarify a given maneuver, it was obviously necessary to limit the number of sequences presented in order to keep the book to a reasonable size. The moves selected are basic to both elementary and championship wrestling.

2. "Panel of Experts"— Thirteen of America's Most Famous Coaches. The information in this book includes the consensus of a group of the country's top wrestling experts on many vital topics such as: the physical and psychological factors in successful wrestling and the characteristics of champion wrestlers.

The panel includes "Art" Griffith (Oklahoma A. & M.), "Cliff" Keen (University of Michigan), Paul Scott (formerly of Cornell College), "Billy" Sheridan (Lehigh University), Henry Stone (University of California), and Henry Wittenberg, America's remarkable Olympic champion of 1948.

3. Physical Factors in Successful Wrestling. Scientific research is the basis for information in this book on development of those physical qualities necessary for success in wrestling. Typical of the research studies conducted specifically for this book is the one on "special foods for competition."

4. Psychological Factors in Successful Wrestling. The psychological aspects of wrestling are treated extensively. The material presented in this area is based upon careful investigation and scientific research. The discussion includes consideration of implications of "Emotional Upset in the Wrestler," "Hazards of Emotional Stress to the Coach," and "Characteristics of Champions."

5. The Role of Wrestling in Education. The authors have made a systematic attempt to clarify the role of wrestling in modern education. Recent research into the nature and development of the human personality has enabled them to discuss authoritatively those forces which mold a healthy personality. The role that wrestling can play in the optimal personality development of young men is explored and discussed.

6. The Administration of Competition. The administration section includes, among other practical suggestions, the procedures, step by step, that should be followed in order to guarantee a successfully run wrestling meet and tournament.

It is our sincere hope that the material which is included in this book will be a source of useful information to wrestlers, teachers, and coaches. We hope that this volume will serve in a small way to enrich the experience of young men and their coaches in the field of wrestling.

A. U.
W. J.

acknowledgments

The authors are grateful to Professor Paul Irvine, Head of the Interpretation Service, Alabama Polytechnic Institute, and his associates, Horace G. Ogden and Joe Quinn, who helped in the preparation of this book. Special thanks are due Phyllis Rea, who did most of the criticism and made many valuable suggestions, and to Jo Salter, whose creative ability in making the drawings was a real contribution.

We wish to thank the following members of the wrestling team of Alabama Polytechnic Institute: Anthony Dragoin, Richard Belfonti, James Johns, Russell Baker, Al Myers, and Jerry Bains, who gave so freely of their time in modeling for photographs.

Much encouragement and inspiration were received from Albert F. Martincic and Anthony Dragoin of the Physical Education staff at Alabama Polytechnic Institute and also from former and present members of the Institute wrestling team.

Appreciation is extended to Bettye Jones for the long hours spent in typing all manuscript.

One of the authors, Arnold W. Umbach, is indebted and grateful to his former coaches, Carl M. Voyles, Dewey Luster, and Joe B. Milam, for their patience, counsel and inspiration.

Sincere appreciation is expressed to the many wrestlers at the University of Denver, Boston University and the University of Maryland who served as subjects for the research reported in this book. Gratitude is also expressed to the competitors in the national tournament of the 1951 N.C.A.A. who were subjected to study and interview. A number of coaches have been most cooperative, particularly William Krouse of the University of Maryland. Final thanks go to James Holland of New York City and to Edson Nyswander of Boston for valuable advice and criticism; and to Dean L. M. Fraley of the University of Maryland for his encouragement and aid in the research ventures.

A. U.
W. J.

To

Our Coaches

Edward C. Gallagher, Oklahoma A. & M.
Granville B. Johnson, University of Denver

contents

chapter 1

wrestling: past and present*

Origin of Wrestling

Wrestling is probably one of the oldest sports known to man. Prehistoric man depended upon his own strength, endurance and cunning for survival. After learning to run and throw it is logical to assume that man learned some form of wrestling. This brutal type of wrestling was his main defense against his enemies and wild beasts. Probably many of the holds and grips that have come to us from antiquity were skills prehistoric man used in daily combat. It is likely that wrestling as a sport grew out of contests between families and neighbors.

Assyrian and Egyptian Wrestling

There is considerable evidence to support the theory that wrestling was highly developed at the dawn of civilization, more than 5000 years ago. In 1938, two slabs were found in the ruins of a temple at Kyafaje, near Bagdad. One was a cast bronze figurine of two wrestlers, each with holds on the others hips. The other was a stone with figures of two pugilists squaring off. These were created by the Sumarians, an ancient people who have long since disappeared.

At about the same time numerous poses of wrestling matches were sculptured on the walls of the temple-tomb of Beni Hasan in Egypt. These ancient records show that wrestling was a highly developed sport at an early date, for they illustrate nearly all the holds of modern times.

The Grecian Period

The Greeks stressed athletic competition not only to train physically fit soldiers; they sought to develop strong, verile, robust and symmetrically built bodies which have never been excelled in beauty. They regarded the wrestler as the best type of athlete, surpassed only by the discus thrower. The Greeks rated wrestling with running and jumping as the most natural form of athletics; it required no paraphernalia, and it provided an excellent method of building muscles and improving health.

*See the references at the end of this chapter

Reference to wrestling appears time and again in Grecian literature. All types of wrestling scenes are shown on Grecian coins and vases. Obviously wrestling was one of the most popular sports of ancient Hellas.

Psychologically speaking, these people felt that wrestling was a civilized art, by means of which ignorance and brute force might be conquered. Pindar tells us that the Goddess Athena taught wrestling to Theseus. The Grecians called Theseus the father of scientific wrestling.

No wrestler was allowed a place in Greek athletic contests unless he was able to demonstrate great skill and gracefulness. It was not enough just to throw an opponent; the job had to be done with great poise and finesse. While brutality and roughness were not actually prohibited, they were frowned upon and, therefore, seldom used. However, a Grecian boy who could not take care of himself in a rough and tumble brawl was looked upon as a weakling.

Pindar and other Greek poets say that the wrestling match between Zeus and Kronos brought about the first Olympic games. On the high peaks above Olympia in 776 B. C., the poets claim, the mightiest of the Greek Gods wrestled for the possession of the earth. The religious festivities and games, held later in the valley below, were to commemorate the victory of Zeus.

The Greeks practiced two types of wrestling which were known as the "Upright" and "Ground." The "Upright" was the most common form. It was held in a pit which had been spaded and sometimes sanded to make a soft surface. The winner had to secure three falls. This style was used in wrestling matches proper and in the pentathlon, and was a type of wrestling similar to our "free style" of today. "Ground" wrestling was staged on a spot which had been watered until it was extremely muddy. The Greeks thought that mud was beneficial to the skin and the muddy surface made the contest less dangerous.

The Roman Period

After the Romans conquered Greece, they took over the supervision of the Olympic games. Under their guidance the games were not a success because the people did not relish competition. The games degenerated into vicious and deadly gladiatorial contests for the amusement of the populace. The Romans never understood the Grecian ideal of sports for sports sake; nor did they care for the Grecian Athletic festivals.

The Grecian culture was so far in advance of Roman culture, that the conquerors became somewhat Hellenized. This was due in part to the fact that Greek slaves taught the Roman youth. One result of this blending of cultures is illustrated by the Graeco-Roman style of wrestling. The Romans' own methods of grappling were blended with the early Grecian style. This Graeco-Roman style is still used in Europe today and is characterized by the fact that holds below the waist are not permitted.

Wrestling in the Middle Ages

The literature of the Middle Ages contains many references to historic characters noted for their science and skill in this manly sport. Wrestling had

achieved great popularity as public entertainment.   Kings established fete days
on which wrestling matches were the feature of the program.   Monarchs of those
days prided themselves on a fine army, but many of them took even greater pride
in having a champion wrestler as one of their subjects.

Wrestling was developed at an early date in Great Britain.   There were
almost as many different styles of wrestling as there were cities.   The most
famous of these styles were the Cornish, Devonshire, and Lancashire.   Annually,
on St. Bartholomew's and St. James' Days these wrestling tournaments were held
in old London.   The champion was given a ram, and others who made a good
showing were awarded a game cock.   The fact that the English monarchs attended
these matches shows the high esteem in which they were held.   Both Shakespeare
and Chaucer wrote poetic descriptions of the feats of outstanding wrestlers of the
Middle Ages.

Throughout the Middle Ages many international tournaments were held.
The nation that won these contests was considered superior athletically.   The
most famous bout of all was the international match between France and England
held at the Field of the Cloth of Gold in 1520.   The English were defeating the
French easily, to the intense pleasure of King Henry VIII of England.   Finally
the French King, Francis I, could endure Henry's gloating no longer.   He leaped
to his feet and precipitated a wrestling match with the English King.   (Thus, no
one can doubt the importance of wrestling during the Middle Ages.)

Wrestling in the Orient

China was probably the first of the Asiatic countries to introduce wrestling
as a sport.   However, even before the Christian era, wrestling had become the
national sport of Japan.   The first wrestling tournaments in Japan were held
about 25 B. C.   These contests are often referred to as "The Wrestling Festival."
The Sumo wrestlers, gigantic monsters weighing between 300 and 400 pounds,
were the feature attraction at all public ceremonies.   They often performed
before the Emperor.   American soldiers who were in Japan after World War II
found that these Sumo wrestlers are still extremely popular in Japan.

Early American Wrestling

American Indians held wrestling matches long before the arrival of Christo-
pher Columbus.   Among the English, Dutch, French and Spanish settlers
wrestling was a popular sport.   Wrestling was frequently the main attraction
at social gatherings and fairs.

Until after the Civil War period, wrestling in the United States was strictly
on an amateur basis.   Following the War between the States, some wrestlers
became such spectacular performers that there was a demand for them outside
their own communities.   At first they were paid only their expenses, but as interest increased, they demanded the full receipts of the gate.   This was the beginning of modern professional wrestling which today is not a sport but a form of
entertainment designed to "give the crowd what it wants."

Modern Olympic Games

Baron Pierre de Coubertin of France, is credited with having revived the first Olympic games of the Modern era.   The games were held at Athens, Greece, in 1896.   However, not until 1904, when the third Olympiad was held at St. Louis, Missouri, did wrestling become a part of the games.   The United States won the first "free style" wrestling tournament.

The Olympics have given a tremendous impetus to wrestling throughout the world.   But no two nations have the same conception of the sport, due to the differences in their cultural and athletic backgrounds.   Therein lies the reasons for so many different styles of wrestling.

Wrestling in Colleges and High Schools

Intercollegiate wrestling had its beginning in this country in 1900 when the University of Pennsylvania and Yale held the first dual meet.   It proved so popular that college wrestling spread throughout the East.   As the result of this popularity, the Eastern Intercollegiate Wrestling Conference was formed in 1904 to draw up a uniform set of rules to govern competition.   The first intercollegiate wrestling tournament was held by this organization in the Spring of 1905.   They have been held annually ever since.   The establishment of the Eastern Conference and the action it has taken has helped tremendously in the growth of wrestling in the United States.

In 1927 the National Collegiate Athletic Association organized the Wrestling Rules Committee; this was probably the greatest step ever taken toward developing amateur wrestling in this country.   Dr. R. G. Clapp of the University of Nebraska served as chairman of the committee for many years.   Due to his very capable leadership and the support of other distinguished members of this committee, wrestling began to grow by leaps and bounds in American colleges and universities.   The committee was responsible for the uniformity of rules and set up a standard code of ethics.

Development of Rules

The authorities of amateur wrestling have never allowed tradition to stand in the way of improvement.   There has been a constant revision of the rules. Our present wrestling bears little resemblance to the style of twenty years ago. New ideas have been tried.   Those that were good have been incorporated into the rules.   The Rules Committee have based their changes on the following objectives: (1) to safeguard the wrestler from injury; (2) to make the sport enjoyable to the participants; (3) to make it interesting to the spectators.

By eliminating dangerous and punishing holds and by improving athletic gear, injuries have been practically eliminated from the sport.   Since the contestant no longer needs to be as cautious as before he can employ greater speed, skill, and versatility.   This, of course, not only adds to the wrestler's enjoyment of the sport, but also makes it much more interesting for the spectator.

Immediately following World War I, high school wrestling began to spread to all sections of this country except the southeast and southwest where it is just beginning to take hold today. In some communities it has become so popular that it carries the entire burden of the athletic department. The rules for high school wrestling are the same as the college rules except for the fact that the bouts are made up of three two-minute periods and the weight classes go as low as 95 pounds.

National Amateur Athletic Union Wrestling*

In addition to college and high school competition, a large number of athletic clubs and Y. M. C. A.'s hold wrestling meets. These contests are sponsored by the Amateur Athletic Union of America. From 1921-1936 C. W. Streit, Jr. of Birmingham, Alabama, served as chairman of the National Amateur Athletic Union Wrestling Committee. He also served as chairman of the American Olympic Wrestling Committee for the following Olympiad: Paris, 1924; Amsterdam, 1928; Los Angeles, 1932; and Berlin, 1936. An excellent job of promoting wrestling on a national and international scale has been done under his very capable leadership.

Until 1948, when the Olympics were held in London, the National A. A. U. wrestling rules had been very similar to the National Intercollegiate rules. Since that time, however, the National A. A. U. has adopted a modified form of the Olympic rules. The reason for this change was to give the American wrestlers an opportunity to compete in contests similar to the European and thus prepare for the Olympics.

These Olympic rules have never been popular with American wrestlers or spectators. At present there is a trend in the United States to adopt a universal set of rules. A majority of the American wrestling coaches urge that these rules should be based on the intercollegiate rules. However, it would be necessary for us to adopt the Olympic rules during the Olympic year in our regional and national championships. Those wrestlers who are best able to adapt themselves to Olympic rules would become members of our Olympic team.

Olympic Wrestling

Every country has its own native style of wrestling. However, in the Olympics all countries use either the Graeco-Roman or Catch-as-Catch-Can style. In the Graeco-Roman style of wrestling, tripping below the hip and all holds applied on the legs are prohibited. A fall occurs when both of a man's shoulders touch the mat simultaneously. The Catch-as-Catch-Can style of wrestling is regarded as a compromise which is accepted by all nations who compete. The wrestlers are permitted to take holds below the hips and, as in Graeco-Roman wrestling, a fall is declared when both shoulders touch the mat simultaneously.

The European approach to wrestling emphasizes the ability to secure locks on an opponent while in a standing position and throw him to the mat for a quick fall. The American wrestling technique puts greater emphasis on take-downs that allow the wrestler to control his opponent after he has been brought to the mat. From this riding position the American wrestler tries to work his opponent into a fall.

---

*See the reference list.

In Olympic wrestling, a fall is declared when a man's shoulders touch the mat simultaneously. This touch-fall tended to make the contestants work very slowly and cautiously. As a result, it has never become popular with the American wrestler or public. Under the intercollegiate rules, the opponent's shoulders must be held continuously to the mat for two full seconds to secure a fall. This has speeded up wrestling, and encouraged the wrestler to take greater chances. It has permitted a wider range of holds, moves, and counters. Consequently, American wrestling is usually considered more interesting to the spectator.

Future Prospects

The present authors believe that intercollegiate wrestling has now developed a highly workable and efficient set of rules. There is little reason to suppose that the near future will see extensive alteration of the present rules. Further improvements in interscholastic and intercollegiate wrestling, such as increased aggressiveness, must come by way of enforcement of the rules and their spirit. It is a serious mistake for coaches to teach their wrestlers to attempt to "beat" the rules. Rule "beating," incidentally, is virtually impossible if match officials are alert and insist upon strict enforcement.

The present wrestling rules are adequate and encourage the best of competition. More coaching clinics are needed, however, so that interpretations may become standard everywhere. More attention, too, should be given to the problem of training competent officials for all matches.

A Tribute to a Great Coach

No history of American wrestling would be complete without a tribute to the late Edward C. Gallagher of Oklahoma A. & M. College. Undoubtedly he will be recognized as the wrestling genius of this century—and was, in fact, the teacher of a number of our panel of experts. He coached the Oklahoma team from 1916 until his death in 1940. Under his leadership Oklahoma A. & M. achieved an incredible record of individual and team championships in one of the nation's toughest competitive leagues. Gallagher was not only the maker of champions: he did more than any other man for the advancement of wholesome amateur wrestling in this country. Back of these achievements was a great man, an inspiring leader and an incomparable teacher.

References and Further Reading

1. Amateur Athletic Union of the United States, *Official Wrestling Guide.*
2. Bowen, Keith E. "A History of Intercollegiate Wrestling in the United States of America." Doctoral Dissertation, Indiana University, 1952.
3. Gallagher, E. C., and Rex Perry. *Wrestling.* New York: A. S. Barnes and Company, 1951.
4. Kenny, Harold E., and Glenn C. Law. *Wrestling.* New York: McGraw-Hill Book Company, 1952.
5. Longhurst, P., and J. B. Pearman. "Wrestling," *Encyclopedia Britannica*, 14th ed., Vol. 23.
6. National Collegiate Athletic Association, *Official Wrestling Guide* (Annual), New York: A. S. Barnes and Company.
7. Rasch, Philip J. "Wrestling," *Encyclopedia Americana*, Vol. 29.
8. Stone, Henry A. *Wrestling: Intercollegiate and Olympic.* 2nd ed. Englewood Cliffs, New Jersey: Prenctice-Hall, Inc., 1950.

the role of wrestling in education

Wrestling is recognized as one of the best of athletic sports in terms of its ability to promote total physical fitness. It is rapidly gaining in popularity as a competitive activity. Wrestling is not only fine exercise, but it is also a fascinating game. A new situation arises with every move the wrestler makes; at one moment he is on the offense, and the next moment he is on the defense. Through wrestling, a boy develops determination, self-confidence, the desire to win and faith in himself.

Athletic Opportunities for Boys of all Types

Practically all the inter-school athletics are dominated by older boys. Many sports have special requirements such as height, weight, or build. But every type of boy can take part in wrestling with good results. No matter how heavy or light a boy may be, no matter how old he is, or what physical type, there is always a place for him on a wrestling squad. He may not be adapted for some sports, but every boy is suited for wrestling. It is as natural for men to wrestle as it is for a duck to swim.

In many of our sports today the boy with a physical handicap encounters great difficulty in taking part. Even men who are blind or with impaired eyesight can participate in wrestling with a great deal of satisfaction. Many of them have achieved distinction in national championships; they asked no concessions.

Body Development *

Every growing boy takes pride in his physical prowess. The desire for physical superiority is so real and deep seated that he is anxious to do everything possible to mold a perfect body. Certainly wrestling has much to offer American youth. Educators, coaches, and sports writers have praised wrestling as being unsurpassed by any other form of athletics for achieving symmetrical body development. Every muscle of the body is put to use; therefore, no one group is over-developed to the exclusion of any other.

In many cases, a boy who reports for wrestling with an under-developed body has built a powerful, graceful body equipped with a strong organic system by the time his school career is over.

It is interesting to review some of the major bodily changes that result from participation in a properly conducted conditioning program such as that which accompanies a wrestling season.

---

*See especially references 3 and 4.

1.   Muscles of the body become larger and tougher.   The growth and toughening of muscles depends upon the amount of work that they do; wrestling requires work of virtually all of the big muscles.   It is for this reason that wrestling develops symmetrical as well as strong bodies.

2.   Bodily coordinations are improved.   Just as fingers become better coordinated with systematic practice on the piano, the entire body becomes better controlled and more capable of skillful, highly coordinated movement with wrestling practice.   Grace and efficiency of motion increase as awkward, inefficient movements are eliminated through practice.

3.   The bones and connective tissues become tougher, stronger and more resilient.   A most practical implication of this type of change is, of course, that the conditioned person is less likely to injure bones or to sprain joints.

4.   The heart becomes more efficient.   We know that the heart rests after every beat while it is becoming refilled with blood for the next beat.   In the wrestler we find that the heart beats slowly.   This means that the heart is powerful in its action, that it pumps the blood with little effort and that it has plenty of resting time.   It is an efficient heart.

5.   Blood circulation improves.   When systematic exercise such as wrestling conditioning is required of the bodily muscles, they need a greater fuel supply carried to them by the blood so that they can do the extra work.   Circulation in the muscles increases, permitting them to work longer and more vigorously without fatigue.

The above types of bodily changes are but a few of the improvements in function and efficiency which make the conditioned wrestler capable of engaging in the most vigorous of tasks or recreational sports and of performing effectively in emergencies.*

Body Control Under Combative Conditions

Wrestling is one of the best of all the sports for the development of balance. An athlete who has developed the qualities of balance, speed, skill and strength certainly has increased his chances for success in other fields.   There is no doubt that many of these qualities are inherent, but at the same time, great improvement can be made by patient effort.   The best way to develop good balance in wrestling is to use correct form in the application of holds.   In order to accomplish this, the wrestler must apply these holds over and over until they become natural to him.   It demands patience and hard work.

The use of weight in balance is a very important factor in wrestling.   The ability to shift one's weight at a crucial moment can be the deciding factor in a match.   This is the difference between an experienced and novice wrestler.   The highly skilled wrestler shifts his weight with considerable poise.   By making his opponent carry his weight, he tires his adversary quickly.

The eyes are not so important in balance.   Even the blind can wrestle and often have remarkable balance.   The most important factor is the development of muscle sense and the internal ear.

---

*References having to do with the effects of exercise upon the body may be found at the end of the next chapter "Getting Ready to Wrestle."

Reaction Time in Wrestling

Players who participate in team games must depend upon vision and hearing for much of their skill.   But the wrestler depends largely on touch and muscular feelings.   His defense is not against a foe whom he sees but against one whom he feels.   He needs quick reflexes.   He must construct his offense play as the contest goes on.   While a football team can lay down a precise campaign an hour before the game, the wrestler must be on the alert as to what his opponent is about to do and instantly plan a counter move while the bout is in progress.   The good wrestler is always thinking ahead of what he is actually doing.   In wrestling we have two personalities on the mat alone, each trying to outwit the other. The one with the quicker reaction time can make greater use of his skills by getting the jump on his adversary.   This marks the difference between a good wrestler and a poor one.

Self-Reliance

Many of our leading educators of today recognize wrestling as one of our best competitive sports. In wrestling they see the opportunity to develop such traits as self-reliance, the desire to excell, and the spirit of conquest, which is the normal heritage of youth.   Nearly all young men want to place themselves in situations where they are on their own, with failure or success depending on their intelligence, speed, skill and strength.   Wrestling is one sport in which the individual is at his best.   He has the opportunity to develop self-expression and self-reliance which may be denied him in team games; he does not need to submerge his personality as part of a team which is directed by someone else.   Once he enters a contest he is on his own.   He is on the mat alone with his adversary. No substitute will appear when his power begins to wane.   Nor can he take time out to discuss his difficulties with his coach; he is fighting his own battle and must make his own decisions.   It is an ideal situation to develop initiative, self-reliance, and the ability to decide upon a course of action.   Even though he may be pressed for time and often in a condition of severe physical discomfort, these qualities will carry him through.   By putting on a good performance the boy develops confidence and self-respect that is his alone—no team-mate can steal his glory.

Developing Courage

Usually an inferiority complex is the result of some unfortunate occurance in early life which has destroyed the boy's self-confidence.   As time goes on he learns to follow the leader rather than take the lead himself.   He goes out for team games, where he becomes merely a part of a machine.

Sports in which the physically handicapped can successfully compete on equal terms with normal men do wonders in eliminating the feeling of inferiority which such people often have.   It is amazing to watch blind boys regain their confidence after successful participation in wrestling.   What combative sports can do for the blind, they can also do for normal boys whose lack of confidence has set them apart from their fellows.   Many boys who had feelings of inferiority have become outstanding wrestlers; it is certain that they have developed initiative, courage, self-reliance and determination, which will carry over into other phases of life.

Social Values*

Too many people are under the impression that the chief benefits of wrestling competition are physical development and endurance.   They fail to realize that one of the greatest rewards of athletic competition is the development of a high regard for personality.   A wrestler learns respect for the talents and traits of the other fellow.   He may hear about all these qualities in a classroom or read about them in a book, but on the mat he meets them face to face.   We not only learn to increase our own skills while working with others; we also increase their skill. At the same time we learn to measure our own skill against those with whom we compete.

A boy who gives himself up to wrestling for all there is in the sport must develop sound habits and good mental health.   He must have a high respect for all the personal rewards of competition.   Weak, unfair, untrained individuals cannot support a healthy society.   If a team is to be strong, the members of that organization must be strong individuals.   They must know how to play hard and well, be able to take defeat and have the courage to come back.

Competition is a way of developing loyalty within a group and between groups.   A wrestling team that has the opportunity of traveling from one college to another or from one state to another cannot help breaking down provincialism and aiding in the process of transplanting ideas.   The closest and most enduring of friendships are commonly found among wrestlers.   Boys learn to meet, know and size up other men.   We need these social attributes today.   Wrestling and athletics in general yield big dividends in body, greater returns in mind and insurpassable returns to society.   The ancient Greeks proved the worth of a nation of athletes.

Wrestling helps to develop the social qualities an individual needs to work with society.   He must learn to think quickly and act decisively, to work out problems for himself and to apply his energy intelligently.   Through training and hard work he develops sound health habits.   He learns to control his temper, nerves, feelings and to demand the respect of his team mates.   He learns to smile when discouraged and to know the meaning of discipline.   These are things which money cannot buy.

Sportsmanship

The very nature of amateur wrestling symbolizes a high level of athletic honor.   The eyes of the spectators, officials, and coaches are focused upon two athletes engaged in a contest.   Being the center of attraction and watched by both friend and foe, they must conduct themselves in a sportsmanlike manner. In all our championships and dual meets there has been a remarkable absence of foul play and ill temper on the part of the contestants.   The objectives of amateur wrestling are to beat your adversary without punishing him and do it with

*See references 1 and 2.

all the skill you command.   If people everywhere would observe the rules of the game and would treat their associates with the same courteous consideration that is demonstrated by athletes participating in wrestling, this world would be a different place in which to live.   The wrestling mat is the laboratory where youth actually practices good clean sportsmanship.   If he does not his team mates will not put up with him.   Wrestling teaches the sort of sportsmanship that stands up under fire.

Wrestling As Recreation

The good use of leisure time has long been an important educational goal but little progress has been made toward that end.   Wrestling can also fit into the picture here.   Recreational wrestling is play, and nearly everyone can enjoy it. Even a man past the half-century mark may still follow the sport he participated in when he was young.   The physical demands are not great because he may quit before he is exhausted.   He will use a greater variety of holds, since he doesn't care whether he is on the bottom or top, he is out there merely for the fun of it.   He tries to keep in good condition and works out about three times per week developing considerable skill in trying to trick his partner.   This is the pleasure he gets from it.   He has no desire to become a champion; his aim is to enjoy the friends he makes and the pleasure he derives from exercise.

References and Further Reading
1. Layman, Emma.   "Contributions of Exercise and Sports to Mental Health," in *Science and Medicine of Exercise and Sports*, ed.   W. R. Johnson.   New York: Harper and Brothers, 1960.
2. Layman, Emma.   *Mental Health Through Physical Education and Recreation*.   Minneapolis, Minnesota: Burgess Publishing Company, 1955.
3. Morehouse, L. E. and A. Miller, Jr. *Physiology of Exercise*.   St. Louis: The C. V. Mosby Company, 1959.
4. Rarick, G. Lawrence.   "Exercise and Growth," in *Science and Medicine of Exercise and Sports*, ed. W. R. Johnson.   New York: Harper and Brothers, 1960.

chapter 3

getting ready to wrestle

The chapters which follow are planned to present the major principles and problems of preparing for wrestling. This information may be compared to the instruction booklets which accompany new aircraft when they are delivered for flight service. Such booklets are prepared after thorough study and testing of the characteristics of the aircraft. They give instructions for servicing and flying which guarantee top efficiency and safety from the machine.

In a similar way, the following information is based upon scientific investigations and upon close observation of wrestlers by the present writers and a group of nationally famous coaches and wrestlers.

Let's Go to the Experts

In spite of the fact that wrestling is one of the oldest of man's sports, the specific physical and mental factors that determine quality of performance are not certain. We know that the successful competitor must have strength, endurance and speed, and that he must know his wrestling skills thoroughly. But if we have two men who are equally strong, equally well trained and have been taught the same amount of wrestling, why is it that one may be successful— perhaps a national champion—and the other may be unable to make the junior varsity team in his school? What specific physical and mental factors determine quality of performance?

The exact answers to a great many of the physical and psychological problems of athletic competition are still unknown. For this reason, in addition to consulting our own experience and the available source material for the facts, we have turned to some of the top experts on wrestling in this country for their opinions. These men have studied wrestling and wrestlers for many years; they have coached some of our most outstanding regional, national and Olympic champions; some of them have produced remarkable championship teams; and some have themselves been extraordinary performers on the mat.

1. Howard Barker—High School, Mason City, Iowa.   Commonly rated one of America's leading high school coaches.

2. Harry Broadbent—Formerly a producer of Southern Conference champions at Washington and Lee; now a top mentor who is coaching at San Diego State College.

3. Fendley Collins—Wrestling coach at Michigan State College since 1936.   One of America's keenest and most systematic coaches.

4. Arthur Griffith—Formerly Coach of Oklahoma A. & M.'s teams since 1940, worthy successor of the late Edward Gallagher.   Olympic team coach in 1948.

5. Granville B. Johnson—A major figure in Rocky Mountain wrestling, both as performer and coach; University of Denver coach for over 30 years, (deceased).

6. Clifford Keen—University of Michigan, sometimes called Dean of the Big Ten; Manager of the 1948 Olympic team; member of the N. C. A. A. Rules Committee.

7. Joseph McDaniel—One of America's all-time great performers in national competitions; formerly, coach at Syracuse University.

8. George Myerson—Great performer and later major leader of amateur wrestling in the Boston area; coach at Boston's Y. M. C. U.

9. Paul Scott—Formerly coach of remarkable teams at Cornell College, Iowa; at present Athletic Director, Davidson College, North Carolina.

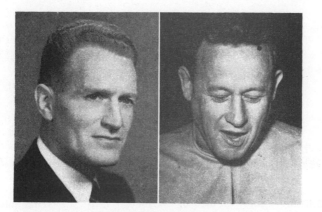

10. Raymond Sparks—Widely respected for his achievements in coaching at Wyoming Seminary, in the Navy, and at Springfield College, Massachusetts.

11. Henry Stone—University of California, Berkeley; Dean of Pacific Coast coaches, (deceased).

Our Panel of Experts

Howard Barker, High School, Mason City, Iowa.

Harry Broadbent, San Diego State College, California.

Fendley Collins, Michigan State College.

Arthur Griffith, Oklahoma A & M College.

Granville Johnson, University of Denver.

Clifford Keen, University of Michigan.

Joseph McDaniel, Syracuse University.

George Myerson, Y. M. C. U., Boston.

Paul Scott, formerly Cornell College, Iowa, now Davidson College, North Carolina.

William Sheridan, Lehigh University, Pennsylvania.

Raymond Sparks, Springfield College, Massachusetts.

Henry Stone, University of California.

Henry Wittenberg, New York City. Although not a member of our panel, Mr. Wittenberg's very interesting contribution may be found in our chapter: "Characteristics of Champions."

It is to these outstanding men that we have turned to test the accuracy of our own findings and observations on debatable questions, in order that our recommendations might be as authoritative as possible. They have generously answered our inquiries regarding what goes into the making of champions and successful team performers. Our experts speak from rich experience in club, scholastic and collegiate wrestling.

Getting into Condition

Many people who know sports rank wrestling as the most strenuous of American sports in terms of total body exertion. We have no proof of this, but we know that competitive wrestling is far too strenuous to be enjoyed by those who are not in excellent condition. Furthermore, our experts are unanimous in their belief that an excellent physical condition helps to build that confidence which is necessary for successful performance in competition.

Many physical factors are involved in getting into condition, but most of these come under three main considerations: food intake, exercise, and rest. These considerations should not be thought of as existing independently of each other because *all three* must exist in proper quality and proportion. In other words, attention to any one of these will not get a wrestler into condition, but careful attention to all of them will.

1. FOODS AND CONDITION*

We sometimes hear coaches complain that they cannot control their wrestlers' diets adequately. "If only I had training tables at my school," they say. Oftentimes our investigations show us these coaches have not taken the trouble to study foods and their effects upon the body very closely. Consequently the

*See especially references 1, 9, 10, 11, 16 and 18.

chances are that boys would not always profit by such diet control even if they had it.   In all events, *let's check with our experts.*

Our experts do not seem to consider the training table as important as one might expect.   Only two of the thirteen specified a desire for three training table meals a day provided by the school.   Seven stated a preference for home cooked meals supervised to avoid certain foods and excesses—Four named the "cooking that the boy is used to" as being best.   It would appear, then, that because a school is not in a position to provide training table meals, its wrestlers need not be at a disadvantage if their meals are wisely selected and well prepared.

Proper eating for wrestlers will come as the result of a cooperative effort by both coach and wrestler.   The well informed coach can furnish his boys guidance in food selection as in other phases of the conditioning program; but it is up to the boys to do the actual governing of their lives in their own best interests.   Wise coaches will not be content to simply lay down the law as to what foods are to be eaten and what foods are not to be eaten.   On the contrary, they will explain *why* they recommend what they do.   If coaches inform themselves of the facts, they will be in a position to give their athletes information which will be of value to them throughout their lives as well as during the wrestling season.   The diet recommended by the experts below is not a mysterious supercharged formula. It is actually a well-balanced diet which should form the basis of any normal diet—athletic or otherwise.

We asked our experts what foods are especially valuable during the wrestling training period.   The following were listed most prominently:

> Lean meat, eggs and other proteins.
> Variety of green vegetables.
> Variety of fruit and fruit juices.

The above three groups were ranked as equals, leading in importance. Cereals, milk, salads and toast were also considered important.

Proteins are of particular importance during the growth period of childhood and early youth, following starvation or wasting diseases and during the building-up period of athletic conditioning.   After a satisfactory level of physical fitness is reached, bodily demands for proteins decrease considerably.

Meats are a major protein source, but research has indicated that other proteins serve equally well in building athletic teams for and maintaining top performance.   Indeed, teams deprived of meat altogether are evidently as well off as teams on a very heavy meat diet.   Comparatively small amounts of meat are sufficient for the wrestler if his diet also includes plenty of such foods as peas, beans (especially limas and soybeans), cheeses, milk, eggs, peanut butter and nuts. Knowledge of this fact is important when meat is inaccessible or very high in price.

Alkaline foods.   The ultimate reaction of most foods in the blood is either alkaline or acid.   Since, in heavy exercise, exceptional amounts of fatigue acids are produced in the muscles, it is desirable to eat foods which cause the alkaline reaction needed to counteract the exercise acids and the accompanying loss of muscular efficiency. The best alkalinizers are the fruits and vegetables, especially the sour fruits (oranges, grapefruit, etc.) and such vegetables as tomatoes, lima beans and white potatoes. Milk is another excellent alkalinizer which is valuable in counteracting the acid formation in the muscles during exercise.

Let us note that the acid and alkaline reactions of which we speak have no connection with the way foods *taste* or with their acidity in the stomach, but rather with their final reaction in the blood. We have stressed the alkalizers in the diet because in the characteristic American diet these foods are not eaten in the quantity that their importance deserves. *

When some people hear that a particular food or variety of foods is good for them, they begin to eat that food in large quantities. This is not necessarily a wise thing to do. For example, beans, we know, are an excellent source of a number of food values; but we also know that in some people beans cause considerable gastrointestinal discomfort—which would be especially unpleasant before an athletic contest. We return, then, to the advice of our experts: the wrestler should eat the foods that he is used to and can digest easily. Since digestive systems and food preferences vary from person to person it is probably unwise for the coach to insist upon an ironclad diet. It is far better to list several kinds of foods that will meet nutritional needs and leave the specific choice to the boy.

Vitamins and Minerals

There is no doubt that vitamins and minerals are extremely important to the proper body functioning. A discussion of them individually will not be made, however, since the well-rounded diet of fruits, vegetables, whole grain cereals and breads, meats and dairy products contains an adequate supply of both vitamins and minerals. A large number of good reference books are available for those wrestlers who wish to look into this matter more closely.

Vitamins and mineral pills are usually not necessary for wrestlers if their diets contain the essential foods. However, in some parts of the country, vegetables which look perfectly normal may not contain the vitamins and minerals that they are supposed to contain.

This condition is usually due to depleted farm soils and is evidently most prevalent in the Eastern United States. Moreover, when fruits and vegetables are incorrectly cooked, they lose much of their value. If there is reason to doubt the quality of the wrestler's diets, coaches may be wise to supplement these diets with daily vitamin pills. (If the body does not need these extras, they are merely passed off and no harm is done.)

Foods Before a Match

Let us now consider foods which seem to be particularly desirable during the hours immediately before competition. As a guiding principle we find that most

---

*See especially references 1, 5 and 18.

of our experts favor having their wrestlers enter a match "with as little food in them as possible, consistent with feeling okay."   Three of our panel members prefer that their men be "lean and hungry" at match time.   None of our experts want their men "comfortably fed" before matches.

We find that most of our experts think that four hours is the minimum time that should be permitted between the last meal and match time.   In individual cases it is possible that two hours may be sufficient, while in other cases six or seven hours, or even more, may be essential.   Factors which should control the wrestler's choice of an optimal interval between meal and match are: 1. the efficiency of his digestive system, 2. how quickly he can digest the specific foods eaten and 3. the extent of his emotional upset preceding the match.   Emotional upset interferes with digestion and may greatly increase the time needed for digestion.   (This problem will be discussed more fully in a later section.)   These factors that control speed of digestion emphasize the individual nature of the conditioning process; what is best for one wrestler, may not be best for another.

In answer to the question, "What foods are *especially* desirable within 12 hours of a match?", our experts named the following: proteins, such as steak, or eggs; easily digested energy foods, such as canned sweetened fruits; honey and sugar; and fruit and vegetable juices.   Other foods listed as important were: baked potatoes, combination salads, toast, vegetables and jello.

Here are two typical menus that competitors might eat between three to five hours before match time:

1.	2.
canned sweetened fruit salad	orange juice sweetened with sugar or honey
small steak or lamb chop	soft boiled eggs
baked potato	toast and honey
green peas	
lettuce and tomato salad	
toast with honey	
sweetened tea	

Few wrestlers choose the heavier meal but the choice depends upon what the individual finds is best for him.   Selection of the wrong foods or over-eating at this time can cause discomfort, lowered efficiency in action, and even nausea during or following exertion.   A large number of champions seem to favor the lighter type of menu.

Effects of Sugar and Other Special Foods on Performance

For many years coaches and athletes have been looking for high energy or other special foods which would improve performance in competition.   From time to time one food substance or another is heralded as being especially valuable to athletes, but virtually all of these substances are discarded when they do not live up to expectations in athletic action.

Sugar, usually in the form of glucose, dextrose, or sucrose, is one of the few substances which has persisted as a "super food."   It stands to reason that since sugar (in the form of glycogen) is muscle fuel, its availability during strenuous activity is essential.   Consequently, most coaches favor relatively large sugar intake up to within a few hours of match time.

In recent years increasing attention has been given to another type of substance which, theoretically and experimentally, might be expected to improve performance.   This substance is any of several blood alkalizers, which, if available in the blood, have been thought to be capable of neutralizing "fatigue acids." These are the acids (especially lactic acid) which are produced as a result of exercise and which are known to be an important factor in fatigue.

Dennig, a German investigator, discovered that large amounts of blood alkalizers, (such as sodium citrate, sodium bicarbonate, and calcium citrate) taken some hours before exercise greatly increased the energy of the individual. At the conclusion of his report, however, Dennig warns that his investigations were under experimental rather than actual competitive conditions.   For this reason he urged caution in supposing that what he had observed would hold true under conditions of actual sports competitions. *

Research conducted very recently at the University of Maryland seems to shed a considerable amount of light on this problem.   An investigation called, "The Relative Effects of Certain Blood Alkalizers and Glucose Upon Competitive Endurance Performance," was conducted in such a way that it was actually possible to see which produced the best results in very strenuous competition: (1) a blood alkalizer, (2) glucose or blood sugar, (3) a combination of an alkalizer and glucose or (4) a placebo (a capsule which contains nothing of significance).

The results of this study showed that it made no difference whether the athletes took the alkalizers, the sugar, the combination or nothing at all. **

It should be kept in mind that the athletes in question were in excellent condition (champions) and had the advantage of a well-balanced, natural diet. Under these favorable conditions it would appear that nature provides the healthy young athlete with whatever fuels and physiological balances he needs in sports competition.   Super foods, it would seem, are not really necessary.

The problem seems to be one of psychology.   If a wrestler *thinks* that he is helped by a certain food, it may be well to permit him to eat it.   A little candy, some honey, an orange or so, etc., will certainly do no harm and may serve to put a competitor in a happier state of mind.

Effects of Pure Oxygen Upon Performance

Since optimal utilization of muscle fuel is dependent to such a large degree upon available oxygen in the blood, it would seem reasonable to discuss briefly the value of employing pure oxygen before, during or after sports competition.

One medical doctor, who is at present serving as trainer for a well-known college hockey team, makes an oxygen tank available to his players between halves of varsity games.   When questioned as to the actual specific value of

*See references 6.
**See reference 10.

oxygen for athletes, the doctor admitted that he was uncertain, but added: "If they think it helps them, it probably helps them!"

Actually, it appears that breathing pure oxygen is in a class with super foods. The healthy, well-conditioned young athlete is probably adequately prepared to inhale sufficient air to oxidize his blood. The chances are that his body simply does not need artificial help. *

Foods Between Matches in a Tournament

Choice of foods between matches in a tournament is a particularly difficult problem. A wrestler may find that exertion in the first match and emotional stress cuts down his appetite between matches. Since body weight falls off rapidly at this time a competitor may go on the mat at a considerable disadvantage unless he eats properly.

In some tournaments there is not much time between matches: consequently great care must be taken to avoid foods which will interfere with performance in the next match. If two to five hours are available, most of our experts seem to favor a meal at this time that is similar to the ones discussed earlier in the chapter. In this case citrus fruit juices and energy foods such as honey, sugar or dextrose in tablet form should be stressed.

Foods to be Avoided

Fried, fatty or greasy foods and heavy starches, such as pastries, are almost universally condemned by coaches.

This does not mean that the human body does not need fats and cannot utilize them effectively. Food specialists tell us that one of the most serious problems in the post-war diet of Europeans today is insufficient amounts of fats. Starches become the faster burning fuel of the body; fats the slower burning ones. Fat is stored in various parts of the body where it also serves as body insulation— for temperature regulation and shock absorption. Our problem then, is not of avoiding fats altogether but selecting them wisely. A reasonable amount of butter, for example, is an excellent source of digestible fat and also includes valuable vitamin A

On the other hand, as match time approaches, it is probably unwise to eat food that is not quickly digested—and fats digest slowly. Therefore they should be almost entirely omitted from the final meal before matches. Pastries and other high fat content foods not only jeopardize competitive efficiency by lingering in the digestive tract, but also make weight control extremely difficult.

Fats subjected to excessive heating, as in repeated frying, and the foods cooked in such fats become more difficult to digest. Evidently these foods be-

*See especially references 1, 11, 15 and 18.

come increasing acid in their effect on the blood.* As we have indicated previously, the wrestler is anxious to build an alkaline reserve in his system to combat fatigue acids; therefore, such foods are undesirable for him.

2.   EXERCISE IN THE CONDITIONING PROGRAM

Proper diet, rest and exercise can carry a young wrestler with a normal healthy body far beyond his expectation of what he can do physically.   All of these factors must be considered; together, they mean growth.   Maximum progress cannot be made if any one of them is neglected.

Strength

Many people believe that a strong person will certainly make a good wrestler. Although this is *not* necessarily true—since other factors are probably of even greater importance—our panel of experts is agreed that the total body strength is a major factor in wrestling success.   This view is confirmed by a leading physical education authority, C. H. McCloy, who has found strength to be the most important element in all motor performance.**

Strength depends upon the ability of muscle fibers to contract against a load. Strength is built by gradually increasing the maximum load against which the muscle is able to contract.   Strength is not built by repeating easy tasks but by performing harder and harder ones.   Wise wrestlers build their strength to a point considerably above what is ordinarily demanded in matches in order that their lifting, thrusting and holding in competition can be accomplished with ease.

Endurance

Endurance is a further step in the development of a good wrestler.   Endurance refers to *how long* a man can wrestle hard without becoming unduly tired; whereas strength refers to *how much* a man can do.

Some of the more important factors involved in developing endurance are:

1.   The ability of the muscle itself to function in such a way that it can contract again and again without fatigue.   (The individual fibers of the muscle work in relays.   Just the number needed to get the job done are working and the remainder resting.   When the working fibers begin to tire, rested ones take over the task.)

2.   The ability of the heart to pump with sufficient speed and power to supply the muscles with the necessary oxygen and fuel by way of the blood stream.

3.   The ability of the respiratory system to supply oxygen in sufficient quantities to the blood.

---

*See reference 5.
**See reference 14.

A good conditioning program prepares the body to handle the strain of vigorous sports such as wrestling. To begin with, the muscle fibers become not only stronger but also tougher. In order to supply the increasingly active and growing muscles with enough blood, new vessels (capillaries) open up in the muscles. This adjustment greatly increases the circulation in the muscles and permits greater and more prolonged action by the muscle fibers.

With progressively increased exercises, the heart, like any other muscle, tends to increase in efficiency and size. An athlete's heart beat is somewhat slower and more powerful than that of a non-athlete. This means that the athlete's heart at rest accomplishes the same amount of work as the non-athlete's but with less effort and with longer rest periods between beats. "Athlete's Heart," which is a large and efficient heart, is actually the best kind of heart to have. This kind of heart is developed primarily by running and other leg work.

At rest, the wrestler's heart tends to pump rather slowly, varying between 46 beats per minute for some to 72 beats per minute for others. The average pulse for wrestlers appears to be approximately 64 beats per minute. Anyone's pulse will vary from time to time, depending upon the exercise that he has had, the amount of sleep that he gets and his emotional state. As we shall see later, emotion may cause his pulse to rise to over a hundred beats per minute before competition.

The wrestler's "wind" is also improved by the conditioning program. The lungs tend to inflate more fully, and the transfer of air from the lungs to the blood becomes more efficient. Thus the blood is provided with improved means for getting rid of its waste products and taking on large amounts of oxygen. In this connection, we recall our discussion of alkalizers (most fruits and vegetables) in the diet. These substances make the blood more capable of disposing of the exercise acids which otherwise hasten the coming of fatigue.

In Fig. 1 you see a comparison of pulse waves—that is, waves which show the vigor of heart action. High waves indicate an ability to perform prolonged strenuous activities.

   A. is the pulse wave of an inactive, badly conditioned person.

   B. is the wave of a great track athlete and is considered very large.

   C. is the wave of a characteristic wrestler who is in good condition and capable of going the full time of wrestling matches without undue fatigue.

The pulse waves of national and world champion wrestlers have not as yet been studied, but it is likely that the best wrestlers have tremendous waves.

There is every indication that the normal heart can respond successfully to wrestling and actually profit by the demands made upon it. These cautions should, however, be borne in mind:

   1. Before entering upon a program of conditioning for wrestling, all boys should receive a *thorough medical examination* in order to make perfectly sure that their hearts are normal. In every known case when a heart has been damaged in athletics, some form of pathology or disease *had already* existed in the heart.

   2. The conditioning program should be graded in difficulty. The season should start early enough to permit comparatively easy workouts at first, and then increasingly difficult ones as time passes. In this connection, our experts

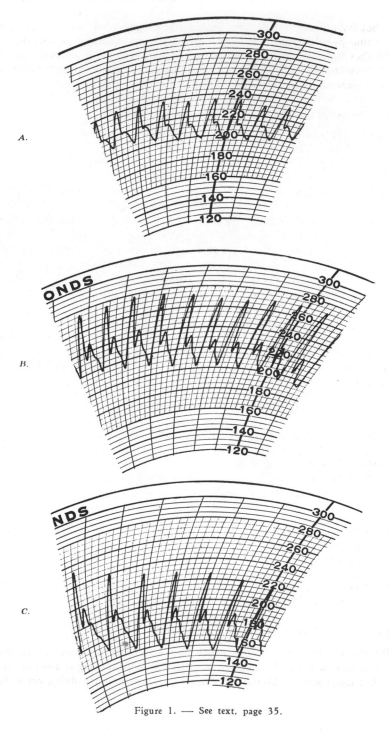

Figure 1. — See text, page 35.

agree that boys should be in the conditioning program from two to five weeks before being permitted to scrimmage.   Most of them consider two weeks sufficient.   They furthermore believe that scrimmage should begin four to eight weeks before the season's first interschool match.   Most of our experts believe that 6 weeks is about right.

Explosiveness

Slow strength is rarely of value to the wrestler.   Explosive strength serves the wrestler best.   The giant Japanese wrestlers ("sumo") grasp their opponents and slowly force them into position.   Our successful wrestlers move in a series of lightening bursts, not grasping and lifting or pulling, but grasping and then exploding to the desired position.   The wrestler who always applies his holds or makes his maneuvers in this way has a distinct advantage; he can frequently make attacks and escapes that won't work for the more deliberate or less explosive wrestler.

Strength and endurance exercises in the conditioning program should be done in sharp bursts to help to develop this quality.   For example, pull-ups should be done with a snap instead of a slow pull.   Run-sprint-run-sprint is better for developing explosiveness than steady distance running pace.

Developing explosiveness has an important psychological value.   If the wrestler always *thinks* in terms of making his moves in an explosive manner, whether in calisthenics, scrimmage or matches, he will find that his explosive ability increases.   Most experienced coaches have seen boys who were explosive in their movements but whose technical skills were inferior, "break the hearts" of and beat more skillful but less explosive opponents.

Balance

"Balance" in wrestling is a quality of extreme importance but is commonly referred to as "intangible" because it is so difficult to define accurately.   We may think of balance as the ability to maintain perfect control of one's position and movements regardless of fast action or surprise maneuvers by an opponent.

The wrestler may develop balance by:

1.   Using correct form in the application of holds.
2.   Learning to be "at home" and effective in every bodily position on the mat and on the feet.
3.   Learning to anticipate—by knowledge of wrestling and by "feel"— his opponent's most likely moves from any given position.
4.   Forming the habit of fighting to maneuver or maintain a given position or ride regardless of his opponent's actions.

Keeping Track of Improvement in Condition

Wrestlers may build their strength and endurance in a variety of ways. Labor and farm work in the summer months will help to bring a wrestler to the season in rugged shape.   Gymnastics (high bar, parallel bars, flying rings, tumbling, etc.) with its body building and co-ordination values, is excellent. Speed and distance swimming will help to prepare the body for the rigors of wrestling. Track and a variety of running games will help to develop that condition of heart and blood vessels which is essential to good endurance. Mountain climbing (especially with a pack on the back), logging and other outdoor activities of a similar kind will promote vital leg strength as well as endurance. Year-round recreational wrestling itself is a good means of helping to keep condition at a high level.

Regardless of the kind of work that his boys have done, the coach needs an accurate record of their body development. There is no excuse for a good wrestler's losing matches because his arms are not strong enough or his arm or leg endurance is not equal to nine minutes of tournament wrestling. Consequently, simple records of the team's condition should be kept so that improvement — or failure to improve — may be studied by both coach and wrestler. Knowledge of status during a learning or growth period is known to be one of the best possible motivators for improvement.

Simple exercises such as push-ups, pull-ups, sit-ups, deep knee bends with a man of equal weight on the shoulders, mile run for time, a dash run or dash with a man on the back—all yield scores which are quickly and easily recorded. When the coach sees that a wrestler is adequately developed by his performance in scheduled matches, he will insist that scores be maintained but not necessarily improved further.

As Our Experts See Conditioning

Wrestling is an excellent conditioner and body builder, but most coaches feel that it should be supplemented by other activities which provide special benefits. But while other sports will help condition the body, only wrestling itself will develop the body in the particular ways necessary for good wrestling. This fact will be attested to by athletes who thought they were in shape from another sport and so decided to go out for wrestling. When they first come out, few such athletes can scrimmage for more than two minutes without extreme fatigue.

We asked our panel of experts about the problem of conditioning. Here is some of the information that they gave us:

1. Conditioning and Confidence: They agreed that one of the best ways of building confidence for competition is to build up excellent body condition.

2. Participation in Other Sports During the Wrestling Season: Only about a third of our panel consider participation in other sports detrimental to wrestling performance. Naturally, they do not want their men injured, nor do they want them to show up for workouts or matches already tired from some other activity. Most of our experts seem to feel that other sports used as recreation provide a refreshing "change of pace." The idea that one sport builds muscles that will not work well in another sport has been greatly overstressed.

Weight Lifting: Coaches are not in agreement regarding the value of weight lifting or weight training for wrestlers. A great many are inclined to be more or less skeptical of weight lifting; but the evidence to date points to some definite desirable effects of lifting.*

We know that although strength is important to wrestlers, there are undoubtedly more important qualities. The idea that the strongest person in a group will make the best wrestler is not necessarily correct. Every experienced observer of wrestling has seen faster, more explosive, more skillful or more clever competitors beat the stronger men time and time again.

It is likely, however, that wise, carefully supervised weight training may have value for "spot" development. For example, a good performer may be at a disadvantage because of a specific bodily weakness; his arms, legs or back may lack adequate strength. Such a man might profit by including in his conditioning program lifting exercises which are selected to strengthen his particular weak regions.

Most of our experts seem to feel that weights may be advantageously used in this way.

3. *Maintaining Peak Condition:* Most of our experts favor tapering off on conditioning activities when a satisfactory level of conditioning has been reached. Two of our panel recommend shortening workout sessions towards the end of the season; two others believe, however, that it is best to maintain an intense schedule throughout the season; several emphasize the fact that the best procedure varies with different teams and individual wrestlers. Let us stress that all of our panel members are experts in this business of wrestling. When there is a difference in their views on a given point, this does not necessarily mean that the minority view is wrong.

4. *When and How Long to Scrimmage:* Our experts feel that there should be from 2 to 5 weeks of conditioning before actual scrimmage. Most consider two to four weeks ample. (Workouts, as we have stated elsewhere, should begin at least four and as much as eight weeks before the first match of the season.)

Scrimmages may be considered dress rehearsals for actual matches. In order to go a full nine minutes in competition, wrestlers should build up to the point where they can go fifteen to twenty-five minutes in practice against several fresh opponents. In addition, some of our experts remind us that scrimmage should also serve as a means of learning pacing; that is, as a means of learning to conserve energy and developing tactical wisdom. Fendley Collins recommends variation in practice match lengths according to individual needs, long matches to develop endurance and short ones to develop speed. **

5. *Number of Matches per Season:* There must be a sufficient number of matches to permit wrestlers to gain experience "under fire." They need to test and learn to control their emotional and physical reactions to the contest, and to develop match wisdom. On the other hand, it must be borne in mind that wrestling is only one of a number of important experiences of young men in school.

---

*See especially reference 13.
**See reference 4.

Neither this sport nor any other should be permitted to completely monopolize their time and interest.

Our panel of experts favor between eight and ten dual matches plus tournaments. This number will probably be somewhat smaller for high school and other young wrestling groups. High school leagues usually set up an arbitrary maximum for all teams involved.

Some coaches try to arrange their schedules in such a way that the season is constantly building towards a climax. Careful analysis of the emotional reactions of wrestlers has shown that the intensity of their excitement before matches varies considerably. This depends upon the wrestler's feelings towards various teams and upon whether he expects a difficult or easy match. Careful scheduling can help to maintain morale and hold staleness to a minimum.

Warming Up for Competition

Warming up should be considered an integral part of any athletic workout. There are two major reasons for this: prevention of injuries and increased efficiency of the body machine.

1. *Prevention of Injuries:* During the course of all violent sports we see performers take heavy blows and falls—and yet, they go on competing without a sign of real damage. The trained athlete is rugged as a result of the toughening effect of the conditioning program on his body, and the warm-up period before each meet. Studies have shown that most athletic injuries take place early in the season before the men are in good condition, and early in a contest before their muscles are adequately warm. *

2. *Increased Efficiency of the Body Machine:* In the combat zones during World War II, fighter aircraft was kept constantly available on "scramble alert." When enemy aircraft was picked up on radar, a scramble was instantly signaled and the pilots got their planes into the air in the shortest time possible for interception. These standby planes had their engines warmed up for at least 10 minutes during every hour that they stood on the field awaiting emergency calls. If this was not done, top efficiency could not be expected of them; cold engines might very well "freeze up" on the take off.

The human body, like a machine, needs to be warmed up for action if it is to perform at top efficiency. Studies of muscle action have shown that the first contractions of a cold muscle are neither complete nor smooth. (Comparable to the roughness of an automobile engine on a cold morning.) As the muscle continues to function, its contractions become increasingly smooth and effective until its peak performance is reached; this level is maintained until fatigue sets in and efficiency begins to fall off.**

---

*See references 15 and 16.
**Although all questions concerning the value of warm up have not been answered, there seem to be no wrestlers or coaches who recommend *not* warming up. See especially reference 16.

Pre-Match Warm-up

How much exercise is necessary before a wrestler can be considered warmed up? Like so many other factors in wrestling, this is an individual matter. Some of our experts suggest vigorous exercise just before a match; others favor more mild warming up. One recommends vigorous exercise only until a sweat is started.

Some great wrestlers like to get their "second wind" before going on the mat. That is to say, they like to pass through the early feeling of fatigue that often comes after a comparatively short period of vigorous exercises. A world champion, according to one of our experts, insists upon running a fast mile before he will get on the mat. Experience has taught him that instead of fatiguing him, this run conditions his body so that he can wrestle indefinitely without fatigue. In a later section we will see what some national and world champions think of warming up.

Wrestlers should experiment with various *kinds* of warm-up activities and *amounts* of warm-up before their matches in order to discover what is best for them. Vigorous massage, skipping rope, running, rolling on the mat, springing into the air repeatedly, "bulling" with a teammate, and a variety of calisthenics are the more common warm-up activities.

3. REST AND SLEEP

The third major factor in getting into condition for wrestling is rest and sleep.

"Fatigue" has been called a major enemy of mankind. Chronic fatigue, that is, fatigue over a long period of time, has been found to be a serious hazard to both physical and mental health. Most young people tend to get adequate rest if they obey their natural impulse to sleep when they are sleepy. It is only when they attempt to engage in too much late evening activity and still get up early for school or work that they fail to get the sleep that they need. If a wrestler is to perform at his peak, he must plan his studies and social activities in such a way that he does not deprive himself of sufficient sleep.*

Most of our experts believe that, "lack of adequate sleep the night before a match actually has a detrimental effect upon a wrestler's efficiency." Consequently, coaches and their wrestlers should give serious consideration to the problem of sleep on the nights preceding matches. Some individuals are of such a temperament that they sleep well every night; such wrestlers should be left alone, since they constitute no problem. Others who normally sleep very well may become sufficiently excited before a match so that they find it difficult to sleep. This problem of emotional upset and sleeplessness will be discussed more fully in the section on emotional upset in the wrestler.

Individuals vary considerably as to how much sleep they need. Indeed, quantity of sleep seems to depend to a certain extent upon such factors as how hard one is working and the adjustments of certain of the endocrine glands, especially the thyroid.** The average amount of sleep needed is usually some-

*See especially reference 7.
**See reference 8.

where between seven and nine hours.   The wrestler should plan his sleep hours in such a way that he is drowsy when he goes to bed at night, feels fresh on getting up in the morning, and does not become sleepy or drowsy during the course of the day.   Excessive sleep, on the other hand, may tend to make a wrestler somewhat lethargic and "lazy."

The Problem of Staleness

Sometimes wrestlers who have been making consistent progress will suddenly discover that they "aren't getting anywhere."   Not only may their progress seem to slow to a stop, but often they appear to be moving backwards in spite of sincere efforts to improve.   This loss of efficiency or failure to improve, is termed staleness.

Symptoms of Staleness—In addition to standing still or actually moving backwards, wrestlers who become stale tend to have a variety of common symptoms, some of which are:

1.   Listlessness: A normally enthusiastic boy may become dull and apparently disinterested.   This listlessness may carry over into loss of interest in food, studies and social activities as well as wrestling.

2.   Weight Loss: Some coaches keep daily weight check charts on all team members, partly in an effort to spot unexplained loss which may indicate staleness in its early stages.

3.   Lowered Efficiency in Spite of Effort: No matter how he tries, a wrestler may find himself being easily beaten by teammates who previously could not stay with him.   Speed and reaction time in scrimmage may be off.

In examining these symptoms of staleness, we are struck by the fact that they are also common symptoms of a variety of *organic diseases.*   Indeed, wise coaches consider the possibility that some disease condition is present and direct the disturbed boy to the school health service or family physician for careful medical examination.   One of our panel of experts spotted an early case of tuberculosis in a boy whose weight record showed an unexplained decline.

Medical examination and other investigation may reveal to the coach that the wrestler is actually not getting enough to eat or the proper foods, that he is not resting satisfactorily, or that he is overly conscientious about conditioning and is working too hard.

On the other hand, it is generally agreed that staleness may be due to psychological factors.   For example:

1.   A boy may not be eating or sleeping properly because of emotional upset over family problems, academic studies, financial worries, or a girl friend.

2.   A boy may be bored with the sameness of the training routine; matches may not occur frequently enough to challenge him, competition in his weight may not be strong enough to drive him to his best efforts, or it may be so strong that his efforts seem futile to him.

3.   A boy may find the unpleasantness of shrinking down to weight week after week gives rise to a psychological reaction in the form of staleness.

Ideally, of course, a coach would prefer to have men who are so strongly motivated to succeed in wrestling that few outside disturbances would be capable of upsetting their psychological balance, and every training session would be received with enthusiasm.   However, the problem continues to exist, even among very promising performers.   What can be done about it?

Getting to the Source of Staleness

Our experts agree that the first thing to do is to look for the specific cause or causes of this unexplained loss in efficiency.   Obviously all cases of staleness cannot be treated in the same manner when their causes may be entirely different. The root of one may be sleeplessness, another may be dietary, another may be financial and still another may be a family matter.

Our experts named the following as the *most* common causes of staleness, connected directly with wrestling.

1.   Too long, uninterrupted concentration on the tough sport of wrestling.
2.   Shrinking down week after week in order to make a weight.
3.   Too long wrestling seasons.
4.   Lack of adequate motivation.

To counteract these particular tendencies towards staleness, our experts recommend the following measures which have to do with the actual coaching situation.

1.   A complete break away from wrestling atmosphere for a day or so after matches.   (Advised by 8 experts)
2.   Shorten daily workout time.   (Advised by 7 of our experts)
3.   Cut down on the number of workouts per week towards the end of the season.   (4 experts)
4.   Devote some days to sports other than wrestling.   (4 experts)

Such recommendations certainly seem reasonable, and one or more of these should have the desired effect of lending variety to training as the season wears on.   In addition, one of our panel suggests giving an occasional day off when the boys are in good condition as a reward for good work.   Another urges careful scheduling of matches and training to point to an emotional climax towards the end of the season.

This plan would place key matches towards the end of the season, where motivation is most needed to counteract staleness.   Athletes are almost always very highly motivated for the first match or two regardless of their difficulty.

The Learning Curve and Staleness

Psychological studies of learning curves have demonstrated that in the course of learning, the learner may occasionally reach a "plateau;" that is, the curve flattens out temporarily and little or no progress is observed.   (See Fig. 2.)

Learning curves also suggest to us that learning tends to be rather slow when a new skill is first introduced.   Then it tends to speed up, perhaps encountering one or more plateaus.   Finally it slows down as an individual gets closer to his top performance.   This slowing down ("law of diminishing returns") occurs as perfection is approached. Bear in mind that plateaus are to be expected in learning, but that they should be considered temporary.

Let us stress in conclusion that staleness, like most other considerations in coaching, is an individual matter. What helps one boy may very well fail for another. Causes of staleness will vary from boy to boy, sometimes being predominantly psychological and sometimes physiological or even pathological.* The difficulty may have its origin in the actual wrestling situation, or it may well involve problems in some other aspects of the boy's life. Most cases may probably be solved by the coach himself if he studies each problem situation with care. Others may require the attention of a physician, guidance counselor or psychiatrist.

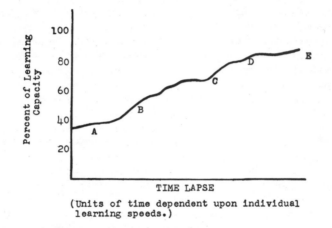

TIME LAPSE
(Units of time dependent upon individual
learning speeds.)

Figure 2 showing a learning curve as it applies in wrestling. (A) when learning begins progress tends to be rather slow. (B) then for a time progress is rapid and easy. Sometimes a plateau (C) is reached in which little or no progress is made. Then, with increased motivation or with the acquiring of more effective skills, (D) progress in learning resumes. Progress becomes increasingly slow and difficult as perfection is approached. ("Law of diminishing returns") (E) Such plateaus may sometimes be interpreted as staleness. When motivation is increased, that is, when a boy has a greater reason for *wanting* to wrestle, or when new and more efficient skills take the place of older and less efficient skills, the curve usually resumes its upward course.

Smoking and Drinking

Young athletes today have to face the problem of smoking and drinking. Parents, teachers and coaches almost invariably condemn these things, especially for very young people. Nevertheless, these same coaches, parents and teachers often use alcohol and tobacco themselves. Young people see this and see that outstanding performers in sports, the arts and military combat frequently not only smoke and drink but boast of doing so. As a result, high school and college athletes as well as other young people, frequently see no good reason why they should avoid these practices.

---

*See references 11, 15, and 16.

Heavy smoking and drinking—and eating—can easily be shown to be injurious to health and physical condition.

There is strong indication at the present time that heavy smoking may be a major cause of such diseases as lung cancer. Unwise use of alcohol, as everyone knows, reduces numerous persons to alcoholism and causes numerous traffic casualties.

But what about these things in moderation? Regardless of the feelings of the authors or of coaches the country over, we cannot in honesty point to scientific physiological evidence to support either those who praise limited use of alcohol and tobacco or those who condemn it for the athlete. Still, we know that moderate users of tobacco and alcohol frequently become heavy users when under emotional stress, when fatigued or when bored.

What do our nationally known wrestling experts say about this problem? All of these experts consider even moderate smoking and drinking during the wrestling season to be either "very detrimental" or "bad." Their grounds for this attitude are evidently both physical and psychological. Thus, they condemn alcohol because it "cuts efficiency" or "hurts team discipline or spirits." These men are among the best in the business; their views are worthy of very serious consideration. Even those coaches who do not object strenuously to moderate drinking and smoking fear the excesses of young people. No one has ever demonstrated that cigarettes, for example, benefit an athlete in any way.

We must bear in mind that competitive wrestling is one of the most exacting of experiences. Anyone who is unwilling to make an all-out effort can have no hope for success in competition. The wrestling season is not a period of easy living or of excesses in food, drink or social activities. It stands, rather, as a severe test of manhood, courage, perseverance and self-discipline. It is literally a consecration to a difficult cause. Our experts seem to feel that a wholehearted effort of this kind leaves no room for laxity which might undermine the central purpose. When two men of equal size, strength and knowledge meet in combat, the outcome of the battle will very likely depend upon the "little" things—little things which, taken together, make for greatness. Serious wrestlers are almost universally unwilling to gamble with their possibilities for success.

Several of our experts report that they never had the occasion to observe the effects of alcohol or tobacco on their wrestlers. These coaches have produced some of the country's greatest teams; their men have evidently learned that conditioning for wrestling is not something to be taken lightly.[*]

Sexual Considerations

Most competitive wrestlers are adolescent boys or young men. During this period of life, sexual interests and curiosities are comparatively newly awakened and quite strong. Young people need guidance concerning sex and its relation to athletic performance. Many older—and often quite successful—competitors are married men; they too need information on this matter. [**]

---

[*]See especially references 9
[**]See reference 12.

There is a traditional idea to the effect that sexual activity lowers men's capacity for hard physical work, including sports competition. One fine high school wrestler withdrew from a state tournament after winning his first two rounds because during the night he had had a nocturnal emission (wet dream). He had been taught that such a thing would rob him of his manliness, so it seemed futile to him to attempt to go on in the tournament.

Our panel of experts seems divided in its views on this subject. However, one of the members points out that he has seen too many married men who were top performers in wrestling and other sports to believe that sexual activity in itself is harmful. Psychiatrists tell us that masturbation, which is common among young people of both sexes, has *never* been shown scientifically to have physically injurious effects. The same is true of nocturnal emissions, which are experienced by most healthy young men after puberty. Because of traditional thinking, however, feelings of guilt do often accompany both of these experiences. The fact remains, however, that unless the athlete has been convinced that they will harm him or hurt his performance, they will not.

Research which is in progress at the present time will help to clarify certain specific effects of sexual activity upon physical performance.

References and Further Reading

1. Bogert, L. J. *Nutrition and Physical Fitness.* 6th ed. Philadelphia: W. B. Saunders Company, 1954.
2. Brouha, Lucien, and T. Radford. "The Cardiovascular System in Muscular Activity," and Brouha, L., "Training," chapters in *Science and Medicine of Exercise and Sports,* ed. W. R. Johnson. New York: Harper and Brothers, 1960.
3. Bunn, John W. *Scientific Principles of Coaching.* New York: Prentice Hall, 1955.
4. Collins, Fendley. "Training for War and Peace through Wrestling," *A.A.U. Official Guide,* 1944.
5. Cureton, Thomas K. *Physical Fitness Workbook.* St. Louis: C. V. Mosby Company, 1947.
6. Dennig, H. "Upon the Increase of Physical Capacity for Accomplishment Through Making Adjustments in the Acid-Base Household," *German Weekly Medical Journal,* Friday, May 7, 1937.
7. Dill, David B. "Fatigue and Physical Fitness," in *Science and Medicine of Exercise and Sports,* ed. W. R. Johnson. New York: Harper and Brothers, 1960.
8. Dunbar, Flanders. *Emotions and Bodily Changes.* 3rd ed. New York: Columbia University Press, 1946.
9. Fraley, L. M., W. R. Johnson. and B. H. Massey, *Physical Education and Healthful Living.* New York: Prentice-Hall, 1954.
10. Johnson, W. R. and D. H. Black. "Comparison of Effects of Certain Blood Alkalinizers and Glucose upon Competitive Endurance Performance," *Journal of Applied Physiology,* 5:577-578, April, 1953.
11. Karpovich, Peter. *Physiology of Muscular Activity.* 4th ed. Philadelphia: W. B. Saunders Company, 1953.
12. Kinsey, Alfred C., *et al. Sexual Behavior in the Human Male.* Philadelphia: W. B. Saunders Company, 1948.
13. Massey, B. H., H. W. Freeman, F. R. Manson, and J. A. Wessel. *The Kinesiology of Weight Lifting.* Dubuque, Iowa: Wm. C. Brown Company, Publishers, 1959.
14. McCloy, C. H., and N. Young. *Tests and Measurements in Health and Physical Education.* New York: Appleton-Century-Crofts, Inc., 1954.
15. Morehouse, L. E., and Miller, A. T. *Physiology of Exercise.* 3rd ed. St. Louis: The C. V. Mosby Company, 1959.
16. Morehouse, L. E., and P. J. Rasch. *Scientific Basis of Athletic Training.* Philadelphia: W. B. Saunders Company, 1958.
17. Seaton, Don C. *Safety in Sports.* New York: Prentice-Hall, Inc., 1948.
18. Van Itallie, Theodore B., *et al.* "Nutrition and Athletic Performance," in *Science and Medicine of Exercise and Sports,* ed. W. R. Johnson. New York: Harper and Brothers, 1960.

emotional upset in the wrestler

The mental state of the wrestler is closely related to the quality of his performance. The coach needs to be as much concerned with the psychology of his men as with their physical well-being. Educationally speaking, wrestling can demonstrate vividly how well young men can react when under emotional pressure. The coach who is anxious to serve his boys will study them carefully and teach them to handle their strong emotions in satisfactory ways.*

Some coaches—and one rather well-known wrestling book—tell boys: "Don't be a coward." This is undoubtedly good advice but it is actually about as effective as ordering an ill person to get over his illness. We must remember that an individual's emotional reactions to life are the result of life-long learning. The years of early childhood are particularly important in this connection. Words of advice regarding "self-control" and "courage" are not likely to alter a boy's patterns of behavior very much. On the other hand, modern mental hygiene tells us certain important things about controlling emotion. By taking these things into account, coaches will improve their chances of leading boys to fullest achievement in wrestling.

Few wrestlers await the coming of a match without strong feelings of emotional upset. To a certain extent experience in tournament wrestling reduces this upset, but even most great wrestlers report feelings of strong anxiety, "butterflies" in the stomach and sometimes fear as the wrestling match approaches. The famous "Strangler" Lewis once told one of our panel members that even after hundreds of professional matches he still felt strong anxiety as he stepped into the ring.

Let us now consider the meaning of this kind of emotional upset, how it affects the wrestler, and what coaches and wrestlers can do about controlling it when it interferes with performance on the mat.

We should begin by understanding that emotional excitement is probably a very important part of getting ready to compete. When a man is in good condition and confident of his knowledge and skill, excitement can bring him to an "edge" so that he may wrestle better than usual. His body literally undergoes certain changes in preparation for the contest. His heart beats faster; unusual amounts of the red blood cells which carry the all-important oxygen make an appearance in the blood; exceptional amounts of muscle fuel (glucose) move into the blood; the blood itself circulates more rapidly through the vessels; and breathing speeds up. In other words, the wrestler's entire body is preparing for the coming action. He is ready to perform at his best.

---

*See references 6, 8 and 9 for detailed discussion of mental health considerations in sports.

It sometimes happens, however, that a wrestler may begin worrying about a coming match several days before it is to take place. He may imagine the coming action so vividly that his body begins to make its emergency adjustments as though the match were actually about to take place. In this way, a wrestler may spend from one to several days in a state of nearly constant readiness for action. His rest may be disturbed because he is not able to quiet down sufficiently to sleep. As a result of this period of excitement, the day of competition may find him tired and considerably below his peak of readiness. This is not necessarily a "bad" kind of emotion; it has merely arrived too soon.

However there are "bad" kinds of emotion which may cut a man's athletic effectiveness considerably. These commonly have to do with an individual's learned habits of reacting when under pressure. Some people who normally function satisfactorily tend to "go to pieces" in emergencies. The term "gymnasium wrestler" is applied to a person who may look like a champion in practice but who performs like a "dub" in an actual contest. These individuals become physically and mentally depressed or uncontrollably agitated when the pressure is on. They are in a state of disorganzation for competition. If the wrestling coach can help these boys to react under stress in a more effective manner, not only will they win more matches but wrestling will become one of the significant experiences of their lives.

One of the important things to remember about strong emotion is the fact that beyond a certain point, as emotion increases thinking ability decreases. This explains why combat troops often cannot remember events in battle and why athletes sometimes cannot recall certain events in a contest.

All coaches are familiar with the excited boy, frequently a sophomore, who performs as though he had lost his ability to think. He fails to see valuable opportunities as they arise, makes bad moves and gives no evidence that he has learned anything in his practice session. Most boys outgrow this "brainlessness" with experience and may never return to it except under great emotional stress. Other boys, who may be very promising as wrestlers, may never outgrow it unless their coaches are able to help them develop a more adequate pattern of response to the contest situation. One wrestler of exceptional speed and strength failed to win a single varsity match—in spite of the fact that he had easily beaten most of his opponents in informal practice matches. In scheduled matches he wrestled like a machine, repeating mistakes and unsuccessful moves again and again. All of his cleverness and ingenuity—his "smartness"—left him when he was under pressure.

How Excited Do Wrestlers Get?

Wrestlers often experience the same symptoms of emotional excitement before a match that soldiers experience in combat. Veterans of the Abraham Lincoln Brigade who fought with the Loyalists in the Spanish Civil War listed the following symptoms: pounding heart and rapid pulse, severe muscular tenseness, sinking feeling in the stomach, dryness in mouth and throat, trembling, sweating of hands, cold sweat, nausea and sometimes actual vomiting and involuntary urination and defecation.*

Involuntary urination and defecation are rarely encountered among wrestlers; however, most wrestlers do experience unusual bladder and bowel activity as contests approach. Sometimes a good wrestler vomits before important matches. Most of the 1951 national intercollegiate champions and runners-up reported "butterflies" in the stomach; and usually fast heart action.

What about scientific evidence of emotional upset in wrestlers? Recent scientific studies have been made to determine a wrestler's emotional reaction as his time approaches to perform. The average normal pulse rate for a wrestler is approximately 64 beats per minute. Even in good wrestlers, this pulse rate often doubles within one-half hour of match time.** Many wrestlers were found to perform best when their heart action speeded up to approximately 100 beats per minute just before they began to warm up for their matches.

Of course we cannot say that all wrestlers' pulse rates should increase by a certain amount before match time, since the amount of increase will vary from boy to boy. Coaches should keep close watch upon the pulse rates of their individual boys as matches approach. If a wrestler's heart rate varies very much from its normal pre-match rate he should receive special attention. If his heart action is slower than usual it is altogether possible that the boy is over-confident or has other problems which are interfering with his concentration upon wrestling. He may be questioned regarding what is on his mind, and perhaps be reminded that it is often the underestimated opponent who beats the champion. Some form of pep talk is often recommended for such over-confidence or indifference.***

If however, the pulse rate is found to be considerably higher than the usual pre-match rate, the boy is probably overexcited. Overexcitation is detrimental to best performance, and it may be due to a variety of causes. The boy may be coming up against last year's champion or some other "feared" competitor; or the opposing team may have a reputation for winning, or the problem may lie within the boy himself. He may have been going too long without adequate rest; his family, girl friend, or studies may be causing his emotional upset which is reflected in unusual sensitivity; he may have lost confidence due to apparent failure to improve in practice or to apparent loss in body conditioning. Whatever the causes, this boy undoubtedly needs reassurance and calming.

Some boys who have been studied have amazing reactions. Some wrestlers' pulse rates actually go over 130 beats per minute without exercise of any kind. Before tournament competition, blood pressures have been recorded at over 230 mm—which is 100 mm higher than what is ordinarily normal for young wrestlers. Such extremes accompany intense emotional upset, which hinders high quality performance. It seems likely that boys who tend to "boil" so violently before athletic events, should not only have the guidance of coaches but also that of

---

*See references 1, 2 and 10.
**See reference 6.
***If a boy has exercised, his pulse rate cannot be used as an indication of emotional upset.

clinical specialists.   In this sense, we may think of wrestling as a valuable means of discovering individuals whose reactions to life and its pressures are inadequately controlled.

Comparison of Wrestlers and Other Athletes

The emotional reactions of wrestlers have been compared with those of several other types of athletes, most extensively with football players. We find that the "normal" pulse rate of wrestlers tends to be somewhat lower than that of football players.   When emotional reactions of the two groups are compared shortly before contest time, the wrestlers stand out as being considerably more excited.

Let us quote briefly from the results of the study in which these two groups of athletes were compared.

> As a group, the football players were aware of comparatively little pre-game emotion.   Most of them did not become particularly excited until just before game time.
>
> As a group, the wrestlers were aware of very considerable pre-contest emotion.   The tendency was for emotion to build up from slight nervous anticipation early in the week . . . to extreme tension and nervousness a short time before actual contact with the opponent. Some contestants reported "nervous anticipation" of the wrestling season as much as a month in advance of the season.   All of the wrestlers dealt with reported that their sleep was disturbed because of anticipation on the nights preceding the matches; two men were unable to sleep more than three hours per night for from one to three nights preceding important matches.   With the exception of one man, the wrestlers found it difficult if not impossible to study during the hours immediately preceding matches.   By match time they usually described themselves as being nervous and tense to an extreme.
>
> In both groups, subjective emotional reactions are seen to be consistent with the objective results.

In spite of the fact that both wrestling and football are combative sports, it is obvious why they should have different intensities of emotional upset.   ". . . Football is a team sport in which individuals work together, assist each other, rest occasionally, receive instructions from a designated person for every play, share in achievement and in failure, etc.; on the other hand, wrestling is a combative sport in which the contestant stands entirely alone, must rely on his own wits, his own planning of offense and defense, and his own endurance and strength for success.   In winning or losing, the wrestler stands nakedly alone on his accomplishment or failure."*

WHAT TO DO ABOUT EMOTIONAL UPSET?

We have pointed out that emotional upset is as much a part of wrestling as conditioning and diet.   The wrestlers show marked excitation as match time

---

*See references 6 and 7; and for further comparison see reference 5.

approaches.   The outstanding wrestler does not permit his emotions to master him—to rob him of his efficiency for performance.   Our panel of experts agrees that "excessive pre-match emotion" (anxiety, fear, extreme excitement) can prevent a good wrestler from being the winner that he should be.   They also agree that coaches can help boys to control this strong emotion.

Following are some considerations which help hold powerful emotions within reasonable check.

1. Physical Conditioning

Virtually all leading coaches agree that an athlete must be in top physical condition to be psychologically right for competition.   If a boy has watched his strength and endurance grow and is certain that he is physically on a par with his opponents, he is very likely to have confidence in himself.   Confidence is a major enemy of excessive emotional upset.

2. Perfection of Skills

Here again is a factor which makes for self-assurance.   Perfectly executed moves in wrestling are the ones that work.   If a boy learns his holds and maneuvers perfectly, he can be confident that they will work.

When a wrestler, who has *perfected* his wrestling skills, becomes so excited or anxious that he cannot think clearly in the early part of a match, he will find that he wrestles *automatically*.   Prolonged and careful training prepares his body to react properly at the right time.   He does not have to think out every movement of an attack or retreat; he simply moves properly as opportunities arise.

Striking illustrations of this automatic performance will certainly occur to every experienced coach.   For example, one All-American halfback received a blow on the head which rendered him "unconscious" in the first play of an important football game.   This football star played the entire game in such a way that no one realized that he had been injured although he did not recover from the dazed condition until several hours later.

Similarly, expert wrestlers have been known to perform well while actually dazed.   Coming to their senses some time later, they have been surprised to learn that they had won their matches.

The ability to move automatically should be considered a basic training to good wrestlers, but it is not a substitute for thinking in a contest.   If two wrestlers are equal physically and are equally skillful, the outcome of their match will depend upon which is the "smarter"—that is, which thinks and plans ahead best in the match.   Strategy and mat wisdom are matters of thinking and are not automatic, since no two matches are just alike.

3. Intensity of the Emotional State

A number of military veterans of World War II have stated that their emotional upset before wrestling matches nearly equaled in intensity what they experienced before actual combat action.

The wise coach will anticipate crises and work to prevent too great emotional upset by building confidence in his boys; by providing them broad competitive experience; by being alert for extraordinary emotionality due to other factors; and by *teaching a realistic philosophy of winning, losing and competing* in general. Developing a satisfactory mental set towards wrestling should begin when a boy first reports to his coach in order to try out for the team.

Beyond a critical point the powerful emotions seem to gain momentum and become virtually uncontrollable; consequently, most outstanding wrestlers seem to take some form of precaution to avoid letting their pre-match excitement or anxiety become too strong. Some of these precautions will be discussed later.

4.   Emotional Upset and Learning

As emotional excitement goes up, ability to learn tends to go down. It is useless to attempt to teach new skills or strategies to emotionally upset individuals. This is especially true of athletes in combative sports. It is useless to attempt to teach most of these athletes immediately before or, in some cases, even as much as a day or more before important contests.

5.   Emotional Upset and Diet

For many years it has been known that sharp emotional excitation can cause the digestive system to stop functioning completely. If a boy tends to become very emotional as a match approaches, measures must be taken to make sure that meals eaten early in the day do not remain undigested in the stomach and intestines.

Undigested food can be a severe handicap to a wrestler. It may interfere with breathing, cause a feeling of discomfort and perhaps nausea.

The kinds and quantities of meals before matches are, as we have emphasized before, highly individual matters. The amount of food that a boy can eat on the day of a contest will depend upon the following factors: 1. how upset he is, and 2. how efficient his digestive system is in digesting food eaten when he is under emotional stress. One boy may safely eat a moderate meal containing a variety of foods a few hours before match time, while another should eat little or nothing until after his match. Food in the stomach as a means of keeping weight up is a handicap rather than an asset. Most of our experts recommend that wrestlers enter a match, "with as little food in them as possible, consistent with feeling okay."

6.   Emotional Upset and Relaxation

The limits of the human body's capacities to perform work are not known. When struggling to remain alive or when otherwise highly motivated, men have accomplished unbelievable feats of strength and endurance. In sports we have every reason to believe that the healthy body can cope with virtually any reasonable demands made upon it. This is particularly true of wrestlers who have been guided to a sound program of exercise, diet—and rest.

Often competitors are unable to rest and sleep properly during the days or hours before contests.   During this period of anticipation and worry the muscles tend to be in a state of tension; the heart and blood vessels may be unusually active.   Satisfactory rest and sleep may become virtually impossible.   Even after severe cases of such disturbances, however, some athletes are able to win national championships.   But after a long period of tension, most wrestlers tend to feel physically drawn and psychologically exhausted before match time.

Some coaches have wondered about using drugs to help certain boys sleep on the nights before matches.   Actually this measure has rarely been taken for fear of injuring the boys or cutting their efficiency.   Experiments are now under way to determine the effect of certain sleep inducing drugs upon physical performance.

Experienced coaches attempt to relieve pre-match tension by recommending a variety of activities to their wrestlers.   Reading and study furnish adequate distraction for some boys; a few can simply relax and go to sleep when they want to.   But the majority of young men seem to profit most by some form of social activity which provides an action outlet for their tension and forces their attention away from their anxiety or permits them to laugh at it.   Table games, group walks, mild sports such as table tennis, and early evening or afternoon dancing will probably be found quite useful.   Movies are popular pre-contest diversions, but they can be surprisingly tiring on the day of a match and are undoubtedly harmful to many wrestlers.

Skillful massage is an excellent way to help relieve bodily tension.   Just as mental upset can cause the body to become tense, relaxation of tense muscle groups has a soothing effect upon the emotions.   Many excited persons drop off to sleep under the hands of a skilled masseur; others merely doze, but massage helps restore them to a more calm state of mind.   Massage should definitely be included among those activities which can quiet the emotions and prepare some wrestlers for sleep.

7.   The Coach and Emotional Upset

As we have indicated before, it is impossible for most people to "reason away" severe emotional upset just as it is impossible for them to reason away digestive upset.   Still, the personality of the coach should be such that he can calm or redirect the excitement of his men—just as animals or small children can be calmed even though they do not understand the actual words spoken to them.

In aerial combat during World War II, it was discovered that commanding officers were, consciously or unconsciously, commonly looked upon as fathers by their men.*   The attitudes and behavior of these officers had an important bearing upon the spirits and conduct of their men, both in combat and at the home base.   Coaches tend to be in a similar position, psychologically speaking. If they win the confidence of their wrestlers, their influence can be tremendous. Former champions who wrestled under the late Edward Gallagher of Oklahoma A. & M. testify to that man's ability to quietly demand the best of them—and to

---

*See reference 3.

get it.   Joe McDaniels, one of American wrestling's all-time greats, tells how Gallagher would quiet him and fill him with confidence as he awaited his turn to wrestle.   What the coach says at such times is not so important as the strength of his personality and the faith that he has inspired in the boys.

To summarize, the coach can reduce emotional upset in his boys in a variety of ways.   Skillful scheduling of a reasonable number of matches, supervising weight loss so as to avoid frequent excessive tapering down, teaching and personally exemplifying a wholesome philosophy of winning and losing and wholehearted striving for a goal, insisting upon adequate preparation in conditioning and skills, knowing when to wrestle a boy in a meet and when not to wrestle him. These are but a few of the ways in which coaches may modify emotional response in the interests of top quality performance and the growth of their boys.

8.   Team Spirit and Emotional Upset

In spite of the fact that wrestling is an individual sport, the importance of team spirit to "mental set" should be emphasized.   Here again, medical studies of aerial combat squadrons demonstrated the importance of a "group spirit" to individual combat morale.   Many thoughtful coaches strive to cultivate team spirit in their wrestlers because they realize that much of an individual's mental strength comes from the group.   Loyalty to the team can call forth the best efforts of many competitors.

References and Further Reading

1. Cannon, Walter B. *Bodily Changes in Pain, Hunger, Fear and Rage.*   New York: Appleton-Century, 1934.
2. Dollard, J., and D. Horton.   "Fear in Battle," *The Infantry Journal,* 1944.
3. Grinker, R. R., and J. R. Spiegel.   *Men Under Stress.*   Philadelphia Blakiston, 1945.
4. Harmon, J. M., and W. R. Johnson.   "The Emotional Reactions of College Athletes," *Research Quarterly,* 23:391-397, December, 1955.
5. Husman, Burris F.   "Aggression in Boxers and Wrestlers as Measured by Projective Techniques," *Research Quarterly,* 26: 421-425, December, 1955.
6. Johnson, Warren R.   "Emotional Upset in the Athlete," *Athletic Journal,* November, 1951.
7. —————. "Emotional Upset in Two Types of Athletic Contests," *Research Quarterly,* 20: 72-79, March, 1949.
8. Layman, Emma.   "Contributions of Exercise and Sports to Mental Health," in *Science and Medicine of Exercise and Sports,* ed.   W. R. Johnson.   New York: Harper and Brothers, 1960.
9. —————. *Mental Health Through Physical Education and Recreation.*   Minneapolis, Minnesota: Burgess Publishing Co.
10. Selye, Hans.   *The Stress of Life.*   New York: McGraw-Hill Book Company, 1956.
11. Ulrich, Celeste.   "Stress and Sport," in *Science and Medicine of Exercise and Sports,* ed. W. R. Johnson.   New York: Harper and Brothers, 1960.

hazards of emotional stress in coaching

At this point it may be well to direct certain information regarding emotional stresses in coaching to the wrestling coaches themselves.

High school and college coaching seems to be one of the most attractive challenges for men in the field of education. It is an opportunity to work on intimate terms with comparatively small numbers of select boys who are eligible for varsity competition. Vast numbers of teachers welcome an opportunity to add coaching to their other duties. Research in physical education has revealed to us much of what athletic sports participation does for young men; but what does coaching do *to coaches?* This question has not been studied extensively in spite of the fact that the welfare of a large number of coaches is involved.*

Coaching is a very strenuous business. Even though the coach may never work out with his men, the job demands a great deal of him, especially in terms of emotional disturbances. Certain individuals should avoid coaching altogether, even if doing so means missing the satisfaction and excitement of the work and turning down extra pay. Many others should analyze their coaching techniques with care so as to cut emotional upset to a minimum.

According to one physician who is also a well-known coach, the consequences of emotional upset are a very real threat to the health of coaches. He has prepared a list of men who have died or have been driven out of coaching because of this stress. It is a punishing situation when a coach must turn out winning teams or lose his job. The effect of this pressure is to force coaches to pay more attention to winning at all costs than to contributing to the educational growth of their boys.

In most regions of the country, the jobs of wrestling coaches are usually not dependent upon turning out winning teams. This is fortunate for both coaches and wrestlers, but it does not do away with emotional upset related to coaching. Men who work whole-heartedly with their boys often become as emotionally involved in competition as the wrestlers themselves—even when they are spared anxiety over job security.

Using techniques quite similar to those employed in studying the emotional reactions of athletes, the reactions of a number of coaches were studied during local competitions and regional tournaments. According to the increased pulse rate, it was found that most of these coaches frequently became as upset as the average athlete. As one coach put it: "The wrestlers are lucky. They only have to wrestle one man but I have to wrestle all eight matches." Anyone who

---

*See references 1, 2 and 3.

has watched coaches during contests will agree that most of them compete from the bench.

Of course, it was impossible to test the coaches before they were physically active because as contests approach, these gentlemen seem to be in constant action.   However, before and during contests their cardiovascular systems became considerably more active than the exercise alone could account for.   During close contests their pulse rates sometimes went up to and above 130 beats per minute, even though they remained seated.   (One coach's pulse rate did not drop below 100 for hours after the meet.)   Their blood pressures were frequently well above 160 mm of mercury.   When the contests were over, these men frequently described themselves as being "worn out," "washed out," or "beat."

Several of our experts listed the following symptoms as indicative of emotional upset that coaches may experience before a contest.   The coach may:

Be unable to sleep well the night before contests.

Have trouble sleeping the night after contests.

Feel irritable or upset as competition approaches.

Feel quite fatigued when it's all over.

Lose appetite on the day of matches.

Feel deeply upset over losses.

Feel that coaching takes a good deal out of you.

(On the other hand, some coaches indicated they believed that they could go on coaching indefinitely without ill effects.)

Some important implications can be drawn from the above discussion.   Modern medicine informs us that emotional upset can be a source of physical as well as mental illness.   In addition, we know that emotional upset can even cause death in individuals whose hearts and blood vessels are in critical condition.   The physician whom we mentioned earlier considers emotional injury worse than physical injury.

An entire area in modern medicine known as "psychosomatics" is concerned with those illnesses that are either started or aggravated by emotional stress. Psychosomatic illnesses vary from heart ailments to severe digestive tract disturbances in which actual ulceration may take place in the stomach or intestines. These illnesses are as real as those caused by germs, and today they constitute one of the major threats to the health of the American people.

A coach frequently is on the job year in and year out, thus subjecting himself to prolonged sessions of varying degrees of stress.   This long term stress has been found medically to be more dangerous than short, intense stress experiences.   In his earlier years a coach may have youthful resiliency that is comparable to that of his athletes.   As time passes he tends to become less well conditioned, accumulate fat and deprive himself of needed rest because of the demands of his work. He becomes less able to stand up under the pressures of emotional stress.   *There is strong likelihood that coaching can then become a serious hazard to his health.*

We would like to venture certain suggestions to coaches and would-be coaches.

1.   Before you go into this kind of work, either on a part-time or a full-time basis, have a thorough physical examination with special attention to the cir-

culatory system.   This check-up is especially important if you have lapsed into that period of middle aged inactivity and careless eating—regardless of your actual age.   The examination may show that coaching is actually not safe for you.

2.   Once in coaching, continue to have periodic medical check-ups, particularly before and after your sport season.   In other words, take as good care of yourself as you do of your wrestlers.

3.   Take seriously such things as nervousness and unusual and lingering bodily pain, especially if they persist and increase in intensity as time passes.   If they do, see a good doctor about them.

4.   If you discover that you have acquired a chronic or incipient illness, or if you find that this work is "taking too much out of you," study your coaching for habits which may be putting undue strain on you.   Modification of these habits may make it possible for you to continue coaching.   For example, many of the details having to do with equipment, the keeping of records, making preparations for home contests or trips, etc., can be handled well by your athletes and other student help.   This tremendous mass of details is often too much for one man to carry and, incidentally, often interferes with the more important business of coaching.

You may also find that you are permitting yourself to become too much carried away by your emotions during contests.   A more realistic philosophy of athletic competition and a little self-control may be all that are needed to make coaching more pleasant and safe for you.   You will also set a better example of mature behavior for your team and other students.

5.   View your sport season as a period of considerable physical and emotional stress and prepare for it—just as your athletes do.

(a)   Adopt a living regime which will provide for adequate rest and sleep; this may be very difficult but it is essential.

(b)   Select a diet that is well-balanced but preferably light.   Overeating and fatness tend to put additional strain on the heart and blood vessels, thus cutting efficiency and increasing possible danger to you.

(c)   Get into good physical shape.   Start gently, follow a graded sequence of exercises until you reach a satisfactory level of condition, and then hold that level.   Although most coaches will probably not attempt to stay with the wrestlers' exercise regime, they can use part of this time for their own lighter routine and should do so throughout the season.   Being in shape is extremely important.

If exercise is done properly, and is accompanied by good diet and adequate rest, it brings the organism to the point where it can do a bigger job with greater ease, a greater sense of well-being and a decreased likelihood of "going to pieces" under the physical and emotional stresses of coaching.

References and Further Reading
1.   Johnson, Warren R.   "Emotional Upset and Psychosomatic Problems in Coaching," *Athletic Journal,* February, 1957.
2.   O'Neill, Desmond.   *Modern Trends in Psychosomatic Medicine.*   New York: Paul B. Hoeber, Inc., 1955.
3.   Selye, Hans.   "Stress and Psychiatry," *Am. Journal of Psychiatry,* 112: 423-427, 1956.

characteristics of wrestling champions

What makes a champion? It is extremely difficult to answer this question with real confidence because champions, like everyone else, are individuals and cannot be made to fit any single mold. However, our investigations lead us to believe that all champions do have certain characteristics in common which largely account for their success in competition. In examining these characteristics, particularly those having to do with attitudes towards conditioning and competition; we are struck by the fact that these very characteristics (painstaking preparation, self-confidence, determination, etc.) are common to successful men in all walks of life. A coach who teaches this fact to his men is helping to provide them with "skills for succeeding" which will apply to all phases of their lives.

For information concerning characteristics of wrestling champions, we have drawn upon four sources in addition to our own observations.

1. Our panel of experts, which includes several great champions of years past and some of the best qualified coaches in the country.

2. Some of America's all-time great wrestling champions including Henry Wittenberg, Olympic champion and seven times national champion.

3. All of the 1951 intercollegiate champions and runners-up.

4. The statistics on certain physical reactions of college wrestling champions—for additional insight into both physiological and emotional reactions of champions.

Our Experts on the Characteristics of Champions

Our panel of experts was asked the following:

1. *What qualities usually distinguish the champion from those who "can't quite make it?"*

Most of our experts consider "mental set," that is the will to win, to be the chief factor distinguishing the champion from the near champion. Obviously, a winning mental set is built upon perfect conditioning and upon knowledge of wrestling; but it is significant that this essentially psychological factor is considered the decisive quality of the champion. Our experts are convinced that a man may have all other characteristics of a champion and still be doomed to mediocrity if he lacks this spark of inspiration.

Other factors which were stressed in answer to this question were ingenuity, self-confidence, explosiveness and perfect execution.*

2. *What is the champion's state of mind before a final match?*

Our experts reported a variety of conditions—"determined," "eager," "confident," "relaxed" and "scared."   Young wrestlers are often reassured when they learn that fear is experienced even by many national champions before competition.   The important thing is, of course, does the wrestler master the fear or does the fear master the wrestler?

In discussing our interviews with the 1951 national intercollegiate champions, we shall see how champions describe their own feelings before match time.

3. *Do champions, by your observation, tend to be very calm or highly excitable?*

Five of our experts answered "calm" to this question, and three of them answered "excitable."   Four stated that they had observed no consistent trend, and one indicated "outward calm but really excitable and ready."   This last answer is well illustrated by champion Tony Gizoni.   (He was voted best wrestler of the national intercollegiate tournament in 1950 and won again in the intercollegiates of 1951.)

There is probably no one temperament that is characteristic of champions· Of the many national champions and near-champions, only one insisted that he *felt* perfectly calm before competition; and this man did not win in the finals. As we have seen previously, strong emotion must be considered to be a part of the readying process which precedes competitive action.   Not only is complete calmness before a wrestling match almost impossible, but it is probably undesirable.   But in the champion emotion does not destroy efficiency.   Joe McDaniels, one of the most remarkable of all American performers, describes his prematch excitement as having been most intense and even painful.   Nonetheless, he is known for his coolness and cleverness on the mat.

4. *Does the champion tend to be team-conscious or independent and self-sufficient?*

Most of our experts feel that the champions tend to be "highly team-conscious and socially inclined."   Some indicated that they had observed no consistency in this matter.

Some coaches have found wrestling an excellent way to make group activities satisfying and pleasant to socially reserved boys.   Wrestling has come more and more to be viewed as a team sport rather than an individual contest.   Wrestling "for the team" helps many boys to put forth a supreme effort in their matches. This team experience has frequently given rise to lasting friendships.

5. *What type of physique does the champion have?*

William Sheldon's work in relating body types with varieties of temperament suggests that persons with similar types of body builds tend to have certain basic personality traits in common.**

*See references 5 and 9.
**See reference 4, for a study of personality characteristics of champions.

Beyond a doubt, virtually all champions are of "medium" build in the sense that *very* slender or *very* chunky individuals are at a disadvantage in all of our more vigorous and violent sports.   Within the medium range, however, our experts feel there is no standard physique that indicates a champion.   Five felt that champions tend to be "between rangy and compact;" two indicated "rangy" and one, "compact."   The remaining five felt there was no general rule.

We should bear in mind that the problem of physiques of champions has not as yet been subjected to extensive scientific study.   It would be interesting to apply the Sheldon classification technique to all regional club and scholastic champions, national finalists and Olympic team members in an effort to determine whether the best wrestlers do tend to conform to a specific type.

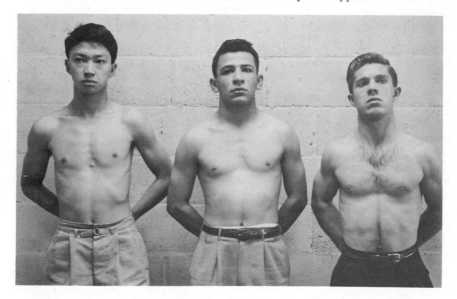

Fig. 3.—Three different body builds, three good wrestlers.   For the wrestler it is not so much a question of what type of build he has as how well he uses the one he has.

6.   *Assuming general good condition, in what part of the body does the champion tend to be especially strong? ***

Ten of our thirteen experts indicated "none specifically—balanced total body."   While insisting upon balanced strength, some of our experts also stressed arms and chest, others the abdomen; one stressed legs and another the back. Certain writers on wrestling have emphasized the importance of neck, arm and shoulder strength, particularly in Olympic wrestling.   A very strong grip is almost universally considered to be an important asset in wrestling.

Future investigations in which the strength of the various body parts of champions is compared with that of average competitors may clarify this question of specific muscular development in relation to championship performance.

*See reference 1.

7. *What type of family background does the champion tend to come from?*

Most of our experts had little to say other than that most champions come from families in the middle economic levels.   This stands to reason when we consider the fact that most boys who attend school, especially college, belong to this economic level.   Three of our experts believe that champions come from any economic level.   Only one goes further, indicating that champions tend to come from homes in which there are close family ties and a rich family life.

A question of this kind gains importance when we consider that mental health and emotional stability in youth and adulthood are dependent to a surprising extent upon the quality of home life in childhood and early youth.   Most wrestlers who "go to pieces" emotionally before competitions come from broken homes or have had otherwise markedly unstable early life environment.   Medical studies of the behavior of large groups of men under combat stress tend to confirm these admittedly limited observations.*

It is true that a few individuals perform well under stress *because of* personality disturbance.**   Hatreds and aggressive tendencies which are generated but unexpressed in the home may make their appearance as extraordinary violence and determination in competitive sports.   But we believe the relatively undisturbed personality is more likely to be consistently effective and less likely to "go to pieces" under the prolonged pressure of a wrestling season.

We raised this question when interviewing the 1951 intercollegiate finalists. Only two of the sixteen men gave their family life experience a low rating, and these two did not win in their weights.   Quite obviously, final conclusions cannot be drawn from this limited group of men, particularly since detailed scientific analysis was not made of each individual's family history.

One of the great challenges of coaching is related to this problem.   Any coach can take a man who comes to him with all of the background and personality traits which make for high quality performance in competition and mold a champion or near champion of him.   But it is the great coach who can take the less gifted boy and, by helping to cultivate maturity of mind and self-mastry, make him into a champion or an adequate competitor.

We are not proposing that coaches attempt to play the role of psychiatrist or clinical psychologist with their wrestlers.   When the coach *observes* faulty adjustment to competition, excessive and crippling anxiety before matches, and decline in performance due to emotional stress, he *knows* immediately that there is a psychological problem.   Common sense tells us that the coach cannot remake the boy's background or even greatly modify his personal life.   He must take the boy pretty much as he finds him and attempt to teach him to meet the stresses of wrestling more skilfully.   If the coach is successful in this, the boy may then be able to make use of these same techniques in other aspects of his life.

---

*See reference 6.
**See reference 8.

8. *What background in physical activity do champions have?*

Eleven experts said that their champions tend to have had previous wrestling experience.   Several also indicated a general sports background (football, swimming, etc.).   Heavy labor experience (such as farming and mining) and gymnastics work were also mentioned.

9. *Do high school champions tend to become your college champions?*

Ten of our experts answered "yes" to this question.

Only persons with considerable wrestling experience realize how complex the sport actually is.   Virtually all coaches who have spent a lifetime studying wrestling freely admit that there is a lot about the sport that they don't know. With so much to learn, boys who have the benefit of high school wrestling under the direction of a good coach ordinarily have a distinct advantage over those boys who take up the sport for the first time in college.   This is also true for club wrestling.

There are, of course, exceptions to the rule.   In spite of the fact that wrestling is very complex, gifted individuals occasionally appear who make a remarkable showing in college and other advanced wrestling without benefit of earlier experience.

10. *As a college coach, would you rather get boys with no experience than boys who were badly coached in high school?*

About half of our experts answered "yes" to this question.   The other half felt that regardless of the quality of previous coaching boys would gain useful experience by merely going out for the sport in high school.

At first glance, it may be difficult to understand why some of our experts prefer no previous experience to previous experience with bad coaching.   Let us analyze briefly some factors which may account for this preference.

Our knowledge of the psychology of learning reminds us that it is usually more difficult to *unlearn* incorrect ways of doing things and then to substitute correct methods than it is to start from scratch and learn the correct way.   To put it another way, a boy who has learned to do a switch incorrectly must unlearn his old habit of switching before he can be relied upon to switch properly in a match.   On the other hand, a boy who is taught to switch correctly in the first place doesn't know any but the proper execution of the move, so can be expected to do it right in competition.   Some promising high school and club wrestlers are not able to unlearn their bad habits; such men are often spoken of as having been "ruined" by their early coaches when they attempt advanced club, college or A. A. U. competition.

Another important consideration is the belief of many coaches regarding beginners: "It's better to know a few holds well than to know a lot of wrestling just half way."   This statement is undoubtedly true but should never be used as an excuse for not teaching boys a lot when they are ready to learn a lot.   If a boy is never led beyond just the basic things of wrestling, he is not continuing to grow; and his future possibilities are limited just as those of a student chemist would be if he were permitted to learn and use only a few basic chemical elements in his experiments.

Many boys who are considered successful high school wrestlers actually know little more than a leg take-down, a ride, a switch and half nelson with crotch pin—after three or more years of high school or club wrestling. Such boys associate successful wrestling with these "over-learned" skills and sometimes, for the rest of their competitive lives when they are under pressure in a match they will return to these basic moves again and again regardless of failure. It is as though their growth were stunted by faulty coaching, and they may be unable to move on to the mastery and use of a broad repertory of wrestling skills which are essential for success in advanced competition. Even though excellent college coaches attempt to increase the knowledge of these limited wrestlers, they are frequently disappointed to find that although the boys seem to be making good progress in practice scrimmages, when the heat is on in a tough match, they swing helplessly back to their old inadequate style. Coaches of beginning and intermediate wrestlers have a definite responsibility to keep the boys growing in regard to skills, for only in this way will they qualify for advanced competition and championship performance.

National Intercollegiate Finalists

The following information is a summary of data gathered from studying and interviewing the finalists in the 1951 national intercollegiate tournament at Lehigh University. The wrestlers were tested and interviewed between matches of the tournament and consequently there was only a limited time available. Certain characteristics of high quality performers are revealed and it is hoped that these may be of value to coaches and would-be champions.

The pulse rates of many tournament competitors were taken. As we have indicated previously, pulse rates before matches (and before exercise of any kind) may justifiably be taken as indicative of the extent of emotional reaction. We find that the pulse rates of these particular national competitors were considerably *lower* than those of ordinary college varsity wrestlers under comparable conditions. While they await theedir turns to wrestle in the preliminary matches, forty men from several of the country's leading teams had an average pulse rate of about 76 beats per minute. Previous studies of "ordinary" varsity teams before dual meets and regional tournaments revealed pulse rates averaging over 90, with some individuals registering 130 beats per minute. The highest rate found in a national competitor was 102 beats per minute.

The implication to be drawn from this data would appear to be that although outstanding wrestlers undergo considerable excitation, their inward turmoil does not tend to be as extreme as that of less qualified groups. The top competitors' excitement does not seem to spill over into that intense emotionality which cripples performance. For example, the average pulse rate of the Oklahoma A. & M. team before competing in the national intercollegiate preliminaries was 73 beats per minute, with three of the team registering in the low 60's. In comparison, the average pulse rate of thirty-five contestants in a regional college tournament (1951) was 99 beats per minute just before warm ups for matches. It would appear to be entirely possible that a comparatively slow, powerful pulse is characteristic of top performers even immediately before competition.

In the finals of the national tournament, the level of internal turmoil, as indicated by pulse rate, was surprisingly low. The average for the sixteen finalists was 70 beats per minute; five of the eight who became champions were in the 60's, and only one of the remainder registered as high as 80.

When interviewed, all but one of the finalists indicated that they felt symptoms of emotional upset of one kind or another. "Butterflies" in the stomach was most frequently named. The symptoms mentioned, however, evidently were not in the extreme form often observed in ordinary competitive wrestling groups. We should add that this observation seems to be in accord with considerable research which has been carried on in regard to the emotions of wrestlers and other athletes. In this research, which involved a variety of physiological measurements of emotional upset, it was observed that in no case were the outstanding performers in *any* sport studied given to extreme emotional reactivity before contests. *

All but one of the finalists reported that they had slept at least fairly well the nights preceding the tournament and the night before the finals. Although the better performers seem to sleep reasonably well prior to competition, a few national champions of the past, such as Edward Collins of New York City, have reported that they were able to sleep very little if at all on the nights before they won in tournaments.

One other question was raised in these short interviews. The wrestlers were asked to rate the quality of their family lives, especially during childhood. The men were assured that their individual answers to this question would be held confidential and they were urged to speak as freely and honestly as possible. They cooperated wholeheartedly and went into considerable detail when they could think of pertinent factors in their personal histories. It is interesting that most of the finalists rated their home lives as being "fair" to "good" in regard to closeness and richness of family ties; an equal number of winners and runners-up (three each) gave a very high rating to their home lives. Only two (runners-up) gave this aspect of their lives a very low rating. When we take into account the fact that individuals frequently find it convenient, when possible, to blame their home lives for their shortcomings, these responses may be significant. Future analysis of the characteristics of champions must certainly take into account this aspect of the question. It is entirely possible that champions are built in the home!

Comments From an Olympic Champion

Henry Wittenberg, champion in the Olympics of 1948, is undoubtedly one of the most colorful and widely respected wrestlers of recent years. Because his competitive achievements have been so extraordinary, and also because his coaching interests have led him to attempt to seek out those factors which contribute to successful wrestling performance, we asked his opinion on the following questions.

---

*See reference 2. Reference 3 points up a similar finding in relation to personality dynamics.

1. *What above all else must a wrestler have to be a champion?*

What, for example, do you consider to be your own most valuable assets?

Mr. Wittenberg: A composite of factors, perhaps as follows:

(a)   strength (explosiveness and power)

(b)   skill (balance, knowledge, timing, etc.)

(c)   condition (endurance plus the ability to pace self)

(d)   speed

(e)   will to win (desire to overcome rival, etc.)

Mr. Wittenberg went on to emphasize that the above factors "*are not necessarily placed in order of importance*, nor is any one factor predominating, but all are interrelated and dependent upon each other."

2. *How do you like to feel before going into a match?*   For example; on edge, perfectly confident, very anxious, entirely calm, etc.

Mr. Wittenberg: On edge.   However, the severity of this feeling has been tempered somewhat by experience.   I feel that every match that I wrestle is important.

(This statement is in essential agreement with those of other champions in wrestling and other sports.   Many outstanding performers consider the excitement that precedes competition to be essential to good performance, in spite of the fact that it may be painful.   It is characteristic of champions that they consider every match they wrestle important.)

3. *Do you sleep well the night before tough matches?*   If you do not rest well, what do you do to calm yourself?

Mr. Wittenberg: I rest well before matches.   I maintain calmness by performing my normal daily routine, but avoid vigorous physical activity.

(Compare this statement with that of one of Oklahoma University's most promising young competitors: "When I get very upset, I concentrate on what I'm doing and shut the coming match out of my mind.   That way I'm able to stay fairly relaxed."   Other national competitors said that they try to think about other things and *keep busy* so that they will not become excessively excited before matches.)

4. *What is the minimum number of hours that you will eat before a match? What are your favorite pre-match foods?*

Mr. Wittenberg: About six hours, and then very lightly.   My favorite pre-match meal is: two soft-boiled eggs, dry toast, tea and sugar, and a swallow of honey—"A hungry dog runs the farthest."

(This great champion prefers the lighter pre-match menu presented in our earlier section on diet.   Such light eating before matches seems to be almost a universal practice among the best wrestlers.)

5. *How important to you is the pre-match warm-up? How vigorous should this warm-up be?*

Mr. Wittenberg: I consider the warm-up to be extremely important. I dress warmly and then do calisthenics and jogging past the point of labored breathing and until a sweat is broken. I like to time my warm-up in such a way that when the match is about to start I am perspiring freely. However, I stop exercising enough before the match that my breathing is at a reduced rate. In any case, I commence warming-up about 15 minutes before my matches, work *very* hard until about 3 minutes before starting time, and then I rest but do not sit or lie down.

(As recommended in our section on warming up, Mr. Wittenberg works hard before matches in an effort to bring himself up to a high level of physiological efficiency. In the process of doing this, he gets what is ordinarily termed his "second wind;" his respiratory and circulatory systems have adjusted themselves to increased and sustained activity, his muscles are hot—and he is ready to go. We would like to point out the likelihood that during the warm-up period, there is also an important psychological warming-up taking place. In the successful competitor, at this time, the physical adjustment for violent action seems to come "into tune" with the mental set or concentration upon wrestling. The readying process is complete. The wrestler goes on the mat at the highest possible level of physical and mental keenness. *)

---

*For a discussion of the profound importance of the psychological warm-up for action, see reference 7.

References and Further Reading

1. Cureton, Thomas K. *Physical Fitness of Champion Athletes.* Urbana, Illinois: University of Illinois Press, 1951.
2. Harmon, J. M., and W. R. Johnson. "The Emotional Reactions of College Athletes," *Research Quarterly,* 23: 391-397, December, 1952.
3. Johnson, Warren R., and Daniel Hutton. "Effects of a Combative Sport Upon Personality Dynamics as Measured by a Projective Test," *Research Quarterly,* 26: 49-53, March, 1955.
4. Johnson, W. R., D. Hutton, and G. B. Johnson, Jr. "Personality Traits of Some Champion Athletes as Measured by Two Projective Tests: Rorschach and H-T-P," *Research Quarterly,* 25:484-485, December, 1954.
5. Kroll, Walter. "An Anthropornetrical Study of Some Big Ten Varsity Wrestlers," *Research Quarterly,* 25:307-312, October, 1954.
6. Maloney, James C. "Psychiatric Observations in Okinawa Shima," *Psychiatry,* 8: 391-399, 1945.
7. Moreno, J. L. *Psychodrama.* New York: Beacon House, 1946.
8. O.S.S. Staff. *Assessment of Men.* New York: Rinehart and Company, Inc. 1948.
9. Sheldon, William H. *The Varieties of Temperament.* New York: Harper and Brothers, 1942.

chapter 7

take downs

The champions of today are clever on their feet and are great take down artists. This is the offense of wrestling. Some of the greatest thrills and cleverest moves in wrestling are the results of take downs.

Some coaches teach their wrestlers to out-wrestle their opponents on the mat. They believe that if the wrestler is careful, ties his opponent up and keeps pushing him around while on his feet, the official will feel that he is the aggressor, thus enabling him to go to the mat at the end of the first period on even terms. These stalling tactics are uninteresting to watch and hurt the sport of wrestling.

Wrestlers must spend considerable time each day on take downs if they want to be good on their feet. The take downs used must be adapted to fit individual build, speed, and agility.

Wrestling on Feet

Good foot-work is very important: A wrestler's feet are not supposed to be planted on the mat. A flat-footed wrestler is slow, easy to get off balance, and quick to tire. If he is light on his feet he is able to move quickly and keep better balance.

He should concentrate on developing these qualities, never cross his feet over; just slide them on the mat and take very short steps. When moving backward or forward, short steps protect him from a heel pick up by his opponent.

A wrestler must remember to keep relaxed, have good balance, and move with speed. When wrestler A is locked up with his opponent, wrestler B, he must keep B under control and at the same time use as little energy as possible. Then, when A gets ready to move he can "shoot" with everything he has, and he can counter his opponent's moves.

Several different standing positions are used. Each wrestler will have to find the position that is most comfortable for him and easiest to maneuver from. Most wrestlers will use either the "open stance" or "closed stance." However, there are a few wrestlers that like to tie up in a special position so they can work their favorite hold, such as the double arm drag set up and the heel pick up position. All these are illustrated below. Most good wrestlers wrestle with their feet parallel or with one slightly forward and about 24 inches apart, depending on the length of their legs. Their weight is equally distributed on the balls of their feet, knees slightly bent. The hips are bent at about a 45 degree angle, with back straight and head up. A person who wrestles "tight" tends to tire more quickly and cannot move as fast as one who keeps loose and has good balance.

Illustrations

All moves will be demonstrated by the wrestler with heavy body outlines. He will be referred to as wrestler A. This will make it easier to distinguish one from the other when their feet, head, and arms become entangled. Note that one wrestler has dark hair, shoes, and trunks.

All holds described will be shown only from one side. However, any hold can be worked from either side.

STANCE

1. Open stance—The stance is the same as described above except that the arms are well extended to protect the legs. The take downs will have to be adapted to this style of wrestling.
2. Closed stance—The stance is the same as described above except that A grasps his opponent's neck with his right hand (note palm of hand is on top of neck) and holds B's right elbow with his left hand with thumb up. A's head is against B's right shoulder. Wrestler B will have the same position on A. Almost any type of hold can be worked from this stance.

SPECIAL POSITIONS

1. Setting up double arm drag—A grasps his opponent's neck with his right hand; throws his left arm up and over B's right arm. He grasps B's right arm just above the right elbow with his left hand with thumb up. A is now in position to work the double arm drag.
2. Setting up the heel pick up—A grasps his opponent's neck with his right hand and then grasps B at the biceps just above the elbow with his left hand, (fingers on top and thumb down). This will force B to take the outside position on A's arm as shown in the diagram. A is now in position to work the heel pick up or many other maneuvers which are available from this position.

STANCE (1) **Open Stance**
(2) **Closed Stance**

SPECIAL POSITIONS (1) **Setting Up Double Arm Drag**
(2) **Setting Up Heel Pick Up**

LEG DIVE

1. Wrestler A assumes the closed stance position; however, it can be worked from any position.
2. Ducks his head quickly and jerks B's head and elbow forward.
3. Drops on both knees with head against B's side. Arms around legs.
4. Brings left leg forward and to outside.
5. Throws head back and into B's side and starts pivoting on right knee. He has a loose grip on legs.
6. Pivots around and moves arm up around waist. Straddles B's right leg.

LEG DIVE

DOUBLE ARM DRAG

1. Wrestler A slides his left arm over B's right arm and grasps him just above the elbow.
2. A brings his right hand across and grasps B just below the right arm pit. At the same time he slides his left hand down to B's right wrist.
3. A jerks B's right arm to A's right and puts most of the power in his right arm using his left hand to guide B's right hand past A.
4. At the same time A moves past B's right side and hooks his right leg around B's right foot. With his left hand, A turns B's right wrist loose.
5. A reaches behind B's right leg with his left hand and swings B around to A's right with both hands.
6. A pulls forward and down with his right hand and swings his buttocks out.
7. He comes on top with his left leg over B's right.

DOUBLE ARM DRAG

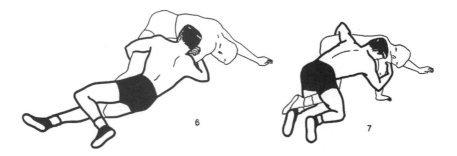

HEEL PICK UP

1. A grasps B's neck with his right hand as B reaches for A's neck with his right hand, A slides his left hand to the inside of B's right arm and grasps B's upper arm.
2. A swings to his left pulling B into him and drops on his right knee. He sweeps mat with his left hand and grasps B's left heel with it.
3. A pulls B's left heel to A's left and at the same time snaps down to his right on B's neck.
4. He keeps pulling up on B's heel and pulling down on B's neck.
5. A turns B's neck and heel loose and goes for inside crotch position, depending on what B does.

HEEL PICK UP

HEAD DRAG

1. A grasps B's neck with his right hand.   As he reaches for B's neck he slides his left hand to the inside of B's right arm and grasps upper arm.   Head should be lower than usual.
2. A holds B's right arm in place with his left hand, as he ducks his head quickly under B's right arm with B's elbow resting on the back of A's neck.
3. At the same time A throws his head back, snapping down on B's neck with his right hand, and swinging behind B.
4. He keeps pulling down on B's neck with his right hand and swings behind.
5. If A has put enough pressure on B's neck he should be behind B and on the mat.

HEAD DRAG

SHORT ARM DRAG

1. A assumes closed stance position as his opponent is putting pressure on him by pushing him around.
2. As B pushes him, A snaps his head to his right through B's head. A's left hand on B's right elbow follows through with A's head. He swings his feet around to B's right leg dropping on his own right knee.
3. A grasps B's right ankle with his right hand. He picks up B's right ankle and steps behind him. A puts his left arm around B's waist.
4. A throws his left leg to the inside and across the front of B's left leg and cuts B to his left.
5. A will come on top into this position, depending on what B does.

SHORT ARM DRAG

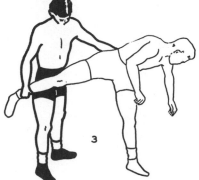

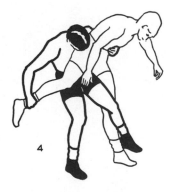

go behind on the mat

Any number of good wrestlers prefer to work down on their knees. From this position they are not as vulnerable to leg holds and they have a much more substantial base from which to operate. It is also a more conservative position than on the feet; the offense is more limited and his maneuverability is restricted. Often wrestlers take this position when meeting an opponent who is clever on his feet. In this case it becomes more of a defense against his moves. However, sometimes a wrestler prefers this position because he is clever on his knees. In either case, a wrestler should learn how to meet this situation because the natural course of the match may lead to it. If he is well prepared to meet this situation, he will have a distinct advantage.

Nearly every hold that is used from standing position can be used down on the mat face to face. However, some are more practical than others.

From this position on the mat A finds it is better to work a little higher than his adversary. This gives A the added advantage as it makes B carry his weight. A keeps his knees well apart so that he will have a good base from which to operate. He should not sit back on his heels too much because his opponent may charge him over. At the same time, he should not charge B too much unless he has B under control.

The following four holds are illustrated because they are the most feasible from this position.

DOUBLE ARM DRAG

1. A grasps B's neck with his right hand, and as B reaches for A's neck, A catches B's upper arm with his left hand. (This shows a different starting position than on take downs.)
2. A slides his left hand down to B's right wrist and grasps B's right arm with his right hand just below the arm pit.
3. A uses his right hand to jerk B's right arm to A's right. A uses his left hand to guide B's right hand past him and swings behind B.
4. He comes into position as shown, his left leg straddling B's right leg and his left arm around B's waist.

DOUBLE ARM DRAG

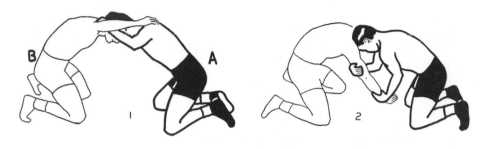

SHORT ARM DRAG

1. A ties up into a closed stance on his knees.
2. As B charges him, A snaps his head through B's head to his right.   At the same time A snaps B's right arm through with his left hand.
3. A jumps behind B and comes into position as shown.

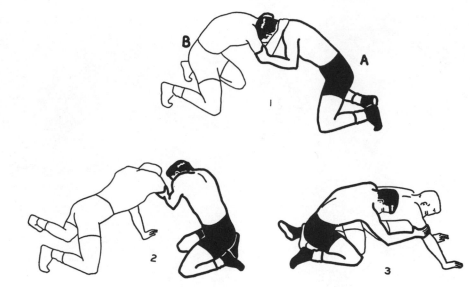

HEAD DRAG

1. A grasps B's neck with his right hand and at the same time keeps B from grasping his neck by catching B's right upper arm with his left hand.
2. A holds B's right arm where it is and snaps head down and under B's right arm pit.   B's arm should be on the back of A's neck.
3. A snaps his head back, jerks down on B's neck with his right hand and swings behind B.
4. Note right hand still holding B's neck.   A is behind and in good position to operate.

SLAP DOWN

1. A grasps B's neck with his right hand and at the same time keeps B from grasping his neck by catching B's upper arm with his left hand.
2. He charges into B forcing him to resist (this is setting him up).
3. A slaps B to the mat hard and gets ready to jump over B's right arm.
4. A keeps pressure on B's neck and right arm with his right and left hand and swings behind B.
5. He comes on top into this position depending on what B does.

SLAP DOWN

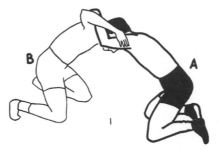

take downs from behind

There are two distinct situations that may develop during the course of a wrestling match in which a wrestler may find himself behind his opponent in standing position. The first occurs when he gets behind while he and his adversary are on their feet. The second occurs when he has control on the mat and his opponent jumps to his feet while underneath; A has to follow B up with his arms locked around B's waist from the rear. This situation occurs more frequently.

When A is behind his opponent on his feet, he keeps his feet about a foot back of and parallel to B's feet. A keeps his arms locked tightly around B's waist and his hands locked tightly together on one hip. This makes it harder for B to unlock A's grip and at the same time gives A more leverage.

If B leans forward, A uses the outside leg trip or crotch pick-up. If he stands up rather straight, A uses the cross-over or back heel. Speed and deception are a decisive factor in these maneuvers.

CROSS-OVER

1. A's feet should be about a foot behind and parallel to B's legs. A's hands locked tightly around waist. Head and grip to one side.
2. He shifts both feet at the same time, throwing his left foot behind B's right and dropping to his right knee.
3. A brings B across his left leg and to the mat. He unlocks his grip and grasps B's right arm with his right hand. A will have B under control.

CROSS-OVER

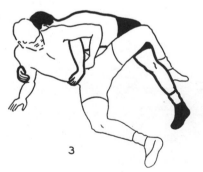

BACK HEEL

1. A is behind his opponent in the same position as on the cross-over.
2. He jumps on the back of both B's heels with his feet as shown.
3. A keeps his right leg straight if he is going to take B to the right, and sits to the mat on his buttocks.
4. He swings B to his right and comes on top of B, breaking his grip as shown.

OUTSIDE LEG TRIP

1. A is behind his opponent in the same position as described in the cross-over.
2. He hooks his right leg over B's right leg shoving him forward.
3. A keeps the leg hooked and shoves B forward with all his weight.   A will come to the mat as shown.
4. A breaks his grip and grasps B's right wrist with his right hand as shown.

CROTCH PICK-UP

1. A is behind his opponent in the same position as shown in the cross-over.
2. He unlocks his grip quickly and places his right hand to the rear and to the inside of B's right leg just above the knee.
3. He raises B up both at the leg and waist just enough to get him off the mat.
4. A drops to both knees keeping head to inside to prevent counter moves. He is ready now to take control of B.

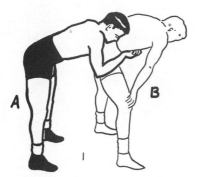

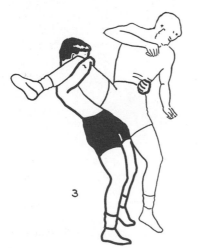

breakdowns and rides

One of the most important areas of wrestling is breaking the opponent down and keeping him under control. The reasons why coaches have placed so much emphasis on this phase is that it is the preliminary to securing a fall. It is dangerous for a wrestler to try to pin an opponent if he does not have the opponent under control. It is a gamble to try to pin a man under these conditions. It turns out to be a rough and tumble affair, either man can be pinned. A's first objective after bringing his opponent to the mat is to flatten him out in a prone position. By getting B into this position A has accomplished a threefold objective: first, he has eliminated the possibility of B's escape by destroying his base; second, A has put B in such a position where he can be pinned; and third, it gives A a chance to relax after shooting hard.

Breakdowns

When breaking B down to a prone position, A uses all the leverage at his command. This not only makes it easier but conserves energy. When A is on top, he must recognize that the underneath man, B has four points of support very similar to a table. The object is to destroy one of these supports. B is well supported when A shoves him straight forward, backward, or to the side. The best way to destroy one of these points of the base is to drive B at a 45 degree angle. This puts him at a disadvantage because he cannot call on his other points of support to aid him. Therein lies his weakness.

Rides

Once B is broken down, A keeps his weight well distributed making B carry it, and at the same time maintains his own balance. This is the best way to wear B down, but A does not make the mistake of using his strength to hold B down. He uses all the weight and leverage he can. This will force B to burn up all his energy. B may become frantic and throw himself open, thus giving A a chance to pin him. One cannot teach a wrestler much about maintaining balance, it comes only after long hours of hard practice.

REFEREE'S POSITION UNDERNEATH

1. The head should be up and looking at the referee, knees well spread with all weight resting on the knees and feet. The arms should be about 12 inches in front of knees and parallel with them, with arms straight.

REFEREE'S POSITION ON TOP

1. One arm should be loosely around the waist with the other hand on his elbow. His inside knee should be back, even with the instep of the underneath man's foot. The knees should be well spread. Head should be up looking at referee.

HEAD LEVER AND DOUBLE BAR

1. A assumes the referee's position on top; hooks his left leg around B's right ankle.
2. A slides his right hand down B's right arm and grabs his right wrist. At the same time, A places his head in B's right arm pit.
3. He drives his head forward, pulling B's right arm backward and to the side. At the same time he uses his left arm around B's waist to pull his opponent at a 45 degree angle on his own right shoulder.
4. As soon as A gets B's right arm back, he shoves it under B and grasps both hands around B's right wrist.
5. A shoves his right elbow forward and puts pressure on the upper part of B's right arm. At the same time, he pries up on B's right wrist. A now has B in a riding position.

REFEREE'S POSITION UNDERNEATH

REFEREE'S POSITION ON TOP

HEAD LEVER AND DOUBLE BAR

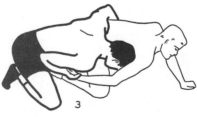

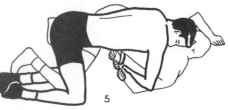

HEAD LEVER AND ARM LOCK

1. A assumes the referee's position on top; hooks his left around B's right ankle.
2. A slides his right hand down to B's right wrist and grasps it. At the same time he places his head in B's right arm pit.
3. A drives his head forward, pulling B's right arm backward and to the side. At the same time he uses his left arm around B's waist to pull him at a 45 degree angle on his right shoulder.
4. A pulls B down to the mat on B's right side. He moves his left arm around B's body and grasps B's right arm just above the elbow with his left hand. A pulls B's right hand up with his right hand. He holds B there, pulling B toward his own back.

INSIDE CROTCH LIFT AND ARM CLAMP

1. A assumes the referee's position on top; hooks his left leg around B's right ankle.
2. With his right forearm A hits B hard across the inside of his right elbow.   At the same time, A lifts B forward at the inside crotch with his left hand.
3. This breaks B's right arm down and at the same time A is lifting B at a 45 degree angle on his own right shoulder.
4. A has now forced B to his own right shoulder, bringing B's right arm under him.   A grasps both of his hands around B's right wrist.   A is now in a good position to keep B on his right shoulder.

FAR ARM AND DOUBLE BAR

1. A assumes the referee's position on top; hooks his left leg around B's right ankle.
2. He throws his right arm across under B's right arm pit and grasps B's left arm just above the elbow with his right hand.
3. A then pulls B's left arm toward his, at the same time, A charges B at a 45 degree angle on his left shoulder.   A grasps both of his hands around B's left wrist.
4. A keeps him on his left shoulder.   A must be careful that he doesn't get over-balanced to B's left or B will roll him.

FAR ARM AND DOUBLE BAR

FAR ANKLE AND NEAR WAIST

1. A assumes the referee's position on top.
2. He reaches across with his left hand and grasps his opponent's left ankle. He places his right arm around B's waist.
3. A pulls B's left ankle forward.   He either breaks B down or keeps him under control.

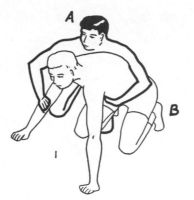

FAR ANKLE AND FAR ARM

1. A assumes the referee's position on top; hooks his left leg around B's right ankle.
2. A shoots his right hand across under B's right arm pit and grasps B's left arm just above the elbow with his right hand.
3. A pulls B's left arm to him and then grasps both hands on B's left wrist.
4. A brings his left arm back and grasps B's left ankle with his left hand.   Then he forces B's left shoulder to mat and keeps it there.

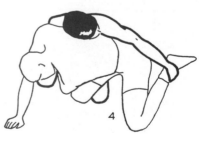

GROIN RIDE

1. A assumes the referee's position on top; hooks his left leg around B's right ankle.
2. Reaches across with his left hand and grasps his opponent's left ankle.   Places his right arm around B's waist.
3. A pulls B's left ankle forward breaking him down to the mat.
4. He puts his left leg around B's left ankle.   B's ankles should be in A's groin.
5. A keeps pressure against B's left instep and at the same time, grasps both hands around B's left wrist.   It doesn't matter which wrist he grabs, just so both hands are on the same wrist.

INSIDE CROTCH RIDE

1. A assumes the referee's position on top, his left leg straddles B's right leg.
2. He reaches across with his left hand and grasps his opponents left ankle. Places his right arm around B's waist.
3. A pulls B's left leg up and toward him. A brings his own left foot up.
4. He keeps pulling B toward him, moving away at the same time. He shoves his left arm into an inside crotch position.
5. He keeps his left elbow on mat in the inside crotch position. Then flattens out and shifts his weight back. If B raises up on his right hand or elbow, A grasps B's right wrist with his right hand and jerks it out from under B.

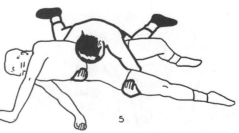

NEAR ANKLE AND CROSS FACE

1. A assumes the referee's position on top; hooks his left leg around B's right ankle.
2. He shoves his right arm across the side of B's face and grasps his left arm just below the shoulder.
3. A reaches back and grasps B's right ankle with his left hand.   B brings his left arm toward A.   B's face should be kept in a cross face position.
4. A pulls B's right ankle forward and breaks B down on his left side.
5. Ties B's arms up and A is ready to go into an inside crotch for a pin.

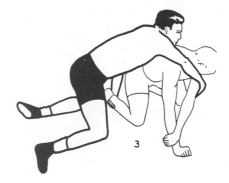

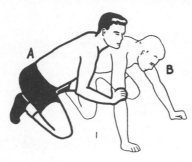

CROSS BODY RIDE

1. Wrestler A assumes the referee's position on top; hooks his left leg around B's right ankle.
2. Puts his right leg to the inside of B's right leg.
3. A keeps shoving it on back through and watches his balance.
4. Hooks his right foot over the top of B's right ankle and grasps B's left ankle with his left hand.   At the same time A hooks his right arm under B's left arm pit.
5. As B rolls, A should be in the position shown in the illustration—his legs wrapped around B's right leg, and his right and left arm holding to B's left arm.

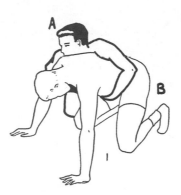

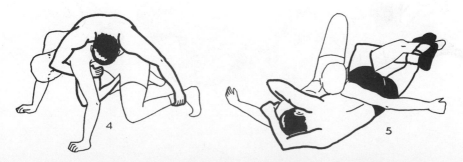

STRETCHER

1. A assumes the referee's position on top; hooks his left leg around B's right ankle.
2. Puts his right leg to the inside of B's right leg.
3. Steps over B's back and shoves his left leg into B's crotch.
4. A has both legs in through B's crotch. Drives forward with all his weight in the small of his opponent's back, at the same time A pulls B's elbow forward with his hands.
5. He lifts both his hands and puts pressure in the small of B's back. Immediately he pulls B's arm up. He will be flattened out as illustrated.

FIGURE FOUR SCISSORS

1. Wrestler A assumes the referee's position on top; hooks his left leg around B's right ankle.
2. Places his left foot through in front of B's left leg and grasps it by the ankle with his right hand.
3. As A pulls his left leg on through, hanging on the ankle with his right hand, he moves his left arm up and around B's chest.
4. A hooks his right leg around his left ankle and A hooks B's ankle then with his right foot.
5. He places all the pressure he can in the small of B's back.   He pulls B forward with his hands prying up on B's elbow.
6. A will be able to flatten B out and ride him.

reverses and escapes

One of the most fascinating areas of wrestling is that of reverses and escapes from underneath. It is a real test of a man's wrestling ability. It requires a keen sense of balance, deception and timing to work out maneuvers from this position. When a particular sequence of movements will effect a reverse or escape he must be able to recognize the situation instantly. He keeps in mind the location of his opponent's legs and arms and just how to use that particular arrangement to get a reverse or escape. He tries to lure his opponent out of position. By a series of maneuvers in rapid succession which force his opponent to block each successive move, he may gain an opening which will give him the advantage. It is best to use a sequence of holds for the purpose of making one hold set up another.

The wrestler must always stay in position where he can control himself and have good balance. He must never let his arms and legs get tied up, because if he does he will be in a bad position and will find it difficult to get out.

If an individual uses many escape variations it is important that he be especially good on take downs. Once he escapes and is behind in points he must secure a take down to regain lost ground. While on the other hand if he reverses he doesn't lose points and stands a good chance of gaining points by controlling his opponent. Often when a reverse is secured it leaves the adversary in a bad situation, which may result in a fall or a near fall. Thus a wrestler using the reverse has a distinct advantage.

SWITCH

1. His opponent is to A's left in referee's position or he could be in one of several different positions to work this maneuver.
2. A takes his right hand as shown in diagram and knocks his opponent's left hand off A's left arm.
3. A brings his left arm across to his right so his opponent cannot counter by catching his left arm.
4. Shifts all his weight to his left hand and right foot, raises his right knee off the mat at the same time.
5. A pivots on his right foot and brings his left leg through to his right. At the same time he throws his right arm over B's right arm and puts it in B's crotch.
6. A leans back on B's right arm and swings his buttocks to the right.
7. A swings his buttocks away from B to get more leverage and takes his left hand and reaches for a rear crotch.
8. Pulls B forward and comes on top.

SWITCH

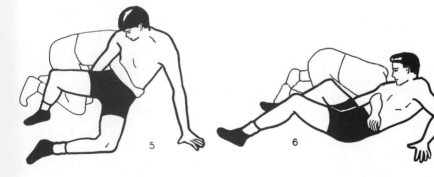

WINGLOCK

1. Wrestler B is on A's left in referee position or he could be in one of several other positions to work this maneuver.
2. A takes his right hand and grasps B's right wrist just above the hand.
3. With his left foot, A hooks B's left leg just back of his knee. At the same time A sits through on his right hip and drops on right elbow. (Very Important)
4. A gives B's left leg a kick with his left foot. He must be sure to keep his right hand on B's right wrist.
5. A throws his buttocks and feet away from B to a right angle.
6. Then A turns B's right wrist loose and turns to left and comes into the position as shown in diagram, depending on what his opponent does.

WINGLOCK

SET OUT *

1. His opponent is riding to A's left with his right arm around A's waist and his left hand on A's left arm.
2. A brings his right foot forward and shifts his weight to his right foot and left hand.
3. A throws his left foot forward as far as he can and drops on his left elbow.
4. Pivots on left knee and elbow and turns and faces B.
5. A then throws his arms out and forward, ready for action.

---

*Also commonly called "Sit Out"

SET OUT

STANDING ESCAPE

1. Wrestler B is riding to A's left with right arm around A's waist and with left hand at elbow.
2. A jumps to both feet, at the same time keeping both hands on the mat.
3. Immediately A grasps B's right hand with his right hand.   He must be sure to grasp all four fingers.
4. Stands up on both feet and grasps B's other hand with his left hand.   At the same time, A hooks his right foot over B's right leg to keep B from lifting him.
5. Pulls B's hands apart and turns and faces him.
6. A must keep himself in a good position to move.

STANDING ESCAPE

1

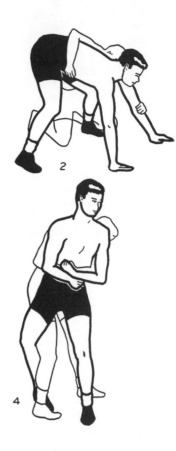

2

3

4

5

6

HIP LOCK ESCAPE

1. His opponent is riding to A's left with his right arm around A's waist and his left hand on A's left arm.
2. A hooks his left arm over B's right arm.
3. Cuts B forward and down.   At the same time A snaps his right knee off the mat, throwing the left hip into B.
4. A pivots on his right knee while B is off balance and comes even with him as shown in diagram.

HIP LOCK AND CROSS FACE

1. Wrestler B is riding to A's left with his right arm around A's waist and his left hand on A's left arm.
2. A hooks his left arm over B's right arm.
3. Cuts B forward and downward.   At the same time A throws his left hip into B.   With the same movement A raises his right knee off the mat.
4. A throws his right arm across B's face and grasps B's left arm just above the elbow.
5. Charges and cuts B under and comes into a whizzer for a pinning combination.

HIP LOCK AND WHIZZER

1. His opponent is riding to A's left with his right arm around A's waist and his left hand is on A's left arm.
2. A hooks his left arm over B's right arm.
3. Cuts B forward and downward throwing his left hip into B.   At the same time A snaps his right knee off the mat.
4. A pivots his left knee putting his right arm across and under B's head and left arm pit.   Note right leg is straight and ready to drive off.
5. Then A throws B over backward to the left.
6. This puts B into a variation of the whizzer as shown in diagram.

HIP LOCK AND WHIZZER

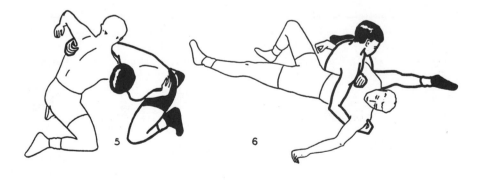

chapter 12

pinning combinations

After a wrestler has developed a good background in the other areas of wrestling such as takedowns, reverses, escapes, rides, and breakdowns, he is ready for pin holds. He must be able to control his opponent before he can safely try to pin him down. This doesn't mean that if an opponent throws himself open that the wrestler shouldn't take the opportunity. By all means he should take advantage of it, but proceed cautiously until the opponent is worn down and then proceed to shoot it.

There are many combinations of pin holds: many are sound while others are freaks and have no place in amateur wrestling. The description of pin holds in this chapter will apply only to those that are fundamentally sound and can be used in a hard match.

BAR ARM AND HALF NELSON

1. A assumes the referee's position on top; hooks his left leg around B's right ankle.
2. Assumes the far arm and double bar position as described in breakdowns and rides.
3. Takes his right hand off B's left wrist and puts a near half nelson on B's neck.
4. As he starts to turn B on his left side, A unhooks B's right ankle with his left leg. Puts pressure on with the half nelson to force B on his side.
5. A forces him completely down on his left side. He shouldn't go any farther until he has completely encircled B's neck with his right arm. The pit of the elbow should now be at the back of B's neck. After the right arm has encircled B's neck, A grasps B's left wrist with his right hand. A now has both his hands on B's left wrist.
6. A keeps driving until he has both of B's shoulders to the mat. A keeps his body perpendicular to B's and his legs spread. This gives A better balance, but he must not let B hook their legs together.

BAR ARM AND HALF NELSON

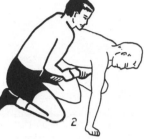

CROTCH AND HALF NELSON

1. Wrestler A assumes the referee's position on top; hooks his left leg around B's right ankle.
2. Shoots his right arm across under B's right arm pit and grasps B's left arm just above the elbow.
3. A pulls B's left arm toward him and at the same time, with his left hand, A reaches for a rear crotch nearer to B's right knee.
4. Picks B up and puts him on his left side.
5. He then takes his right arm and places a half nelson on B and then slides it on around his neck until it is completely encircled.   A grasps B's left arm with his right hand.   At the same time he changes his left hand from a rear crotch to an inside crotch.
6. A must keep his body perpendicular to B's and his feet well spread.   If B turns toward him, he drives B's shoulders back to the mat.   If B tries to turn away from him, A flattens out on him.

CROTCH AND HALF NELSON

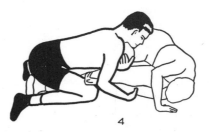

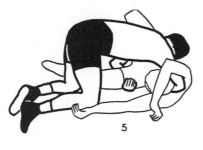

CHICKEN WING AND HALF NELSON

1. Starting from a near double bar arm ride, A straddles B's right leg.
2. Takes his right hand off B's right wrist and shoves it up under B's right forearm until his right hand is well upon B's shoulder.
3. Then A crosses over to B's left side, being sure to keep a hold on B's right wrist with his hand.
4. A takes left hand off B's right wrist and places a half nelson on his neck. Gradually A turns B on his shoulders but not on his back.
5. A steps his right leg across B's head to where he straddles B's head.   A is on his knees.   B should now be standing on his head and shoulders.   A must be sure his legs are well spread and buttock high to give him good balance.

ARM LOCK AND BODY PRESS

1. A assumes the referee's position on top; hooks his left leg around B's right ankle.
2. He takes the same position on his opponent as he did on the head lever and double bar, breaking B down as shown.
3. Then A pulls B's right arm close to B's right side. A slides his left arm around B's waist until he can grasp B's right arm just above the elbow with his left hand.
4. Then he crosses over to B's left side and pulls B's right arm up into a right angle position on his opponent's back.
5. Now A charges him until he has forced B on his back.   If B turns away from him, A flattens out and if B turns into him, A drives B onto his back.

THREE-QUARTER NELSON

1. Wrestler A assumes referee's position on top; hooks his left leg around B's right ankle.
2. Brings his left arm from around B's waist and puts it through from under B's right side up under his chest so it comes out on the left side of B's neck.   A takes his right hand and grasps his own left hand on the back of B's neck.
3. Clamps down on B's neck keeping his left leg hooked around B's right ankle, at the same time pulling B's right foot toward him.
4. A keeps pulling B's right leg toward him until he has B's head between B's legs.   A shifts his own weight back to keep B from kicking him on over. This gives him better balance.   B's shoulders should be flat.

DOUBLE DOUBLE

1. This pin hold is best taken when the opponent takes a hip lock position on him.   Note that A has B's right leg hooked with his left leg and that B has his right arm hooked over A's left arm around B's waist.
2. From this position A throws his right arm up and across the back of B's neck keeping leg hooked.
3. A brings his left arm up from around B's waist and grasps his own right hand with his left hand, putting pressure on back of B's neck.
4. A forces B's head down and under until B is on his shoulders.   He keeps B's leg hooked and shifts his own weight back to the end of B's right foot to get better leverage and balance.

counters for take downs

It is important that a wrestler know the counters to the most common take downs if he expects to have a defense for his opponent. The smart thing for A to do is to keep his opponent off balance so he cannot get A set up for his favorite take down. The first prerequisite in taking advantage of counters is to be quick to react to the opponent's moves. This makes it much easier to outmaneuver him.

This chapter will discuss only the counters that are most frequently used against the take downs that are illustrated in this book.

COUNTERS TO LEG DIVES

FARTHER LEG AND CROSS FACE

1. As soon as his opponent has dropped under him on both knees, A flattens out on him. He keeps legs straight and spread, making B carry all his weight. Reaches across with both hands and grasps farther ankle with both hands.
2. After A has B under control, he takes right hand off B's ankle and cross face him by grasping B's arm just above his left elbow.
3. A snaps his own leg back by pulling on B's left ankle and left arm.
4. Once his legs are free, A swings behind B and straddles his right leg. He now has B in a riding position of a cross face and farther ankle.

COUNTERS TO LEG DIVES: FARTHER LEG AND CROSS FACE

HIP LOCK AND CROSS-FACE

1. As soon as his opponent has dropped under him on both knees, A flattens out on him. Keeps legs straight and spread out, making B carry all his weight. A reaches back with his left arm and places it under B's right arm pit and grasps the back of his own left leg.
2. A cuts B forward with his left arm by snapping his own right leg straight and free of B's left arm.   Note legs are well spread to give good balance.
3. A cross-faces B with his right arm and grasps B's left arm just above the elbow.
4. He cuts B under by driving into him and A will have B on his side and in position for a pin hold.

COUNTERS TO LEG DIVES: HIP LOCK AND CROSS FACE

COUNTERS TO DOUBLE ARM DRAG

CROSS-OVER

1. When B gets into the position shown in this diagram, A gets ready to cross-over.
2. A steps across with the right leg followed by the left leg.
3. Both legs should be perpendicular to B's body as shown in this diagram.

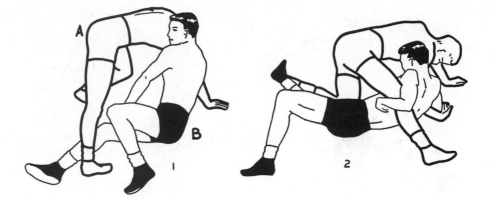

COUNTER DRAG

1. When B is in this position on the double arm drag, A gets ready to bring his right hand up.
2. Grasps B's right arm just below the shoulder pit with his right hand as shown. A starts to pivot on his right foot by placing his weight on it.
3. A sets through and jerks B to the right and past him.   A keeps his own left arm up in case B tries to counter by crossing over.

COUNTER TO HEEL PICK UP

ARM LIFT

1. As his opponent drops to his knees A hooks his left arm under B's right arm.
2. When B reaches for A's left foot with his left hand, A pries up on B's right arm and grasps B's left arm just above the elbow with his right hand.
3. A snaps his legs back and cuts B under into a variation of the whizzer.   A keeps body perpendicular by sitting on his left hip with feet spread to keep good balance.

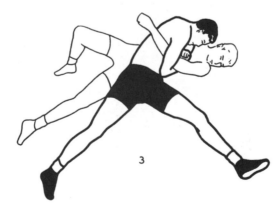

COUNTER TO HEAD DRAG

NEAR WING AND CROSS-OVER

1. As B ducks his head under A's right arm to go behind, A hooks his right arm around B's right arm.
2. Jerks down and brings B's right shoulder and hip to the mat, at the same time throwing his own right leg high over B, followed by his left leg.
3. This should put A perpendicular to B's body with legs well spread. If A can maneuver B correctly he may get a pin out of this move.

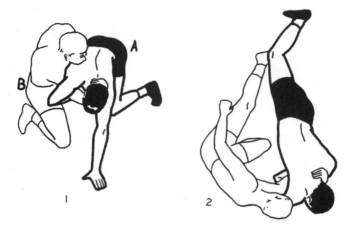

COUNTER FOR SHORT ARM DRAG

SWITCH

1. After B has caught A's foot and picks it up, A turns toward him and grasps B's right wrist with his left hand.   At the same time, throwing his right arm up over B's back.
2. A throws his right arm down over B's left arm and places his right hand in B's crotch.
3. Sits down and swings out to his left to get better leverage on B.
4. If necessary, A uses both hands to apply more leverage and swings his buttock to his left to get more power.   Note that he has freed his right foot from B.
5. Swings wide and comes on top as shown in the illustration.

COUNTER FOR SHORT ARM DRAG: SWITCH

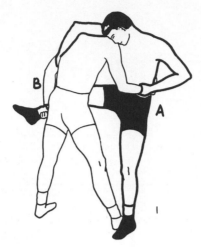

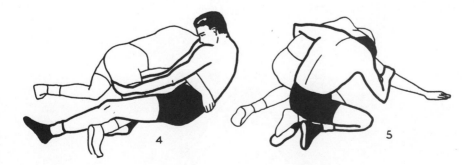

counters for go behinds on the mat

The same maneuvers that are successful for takedowns can be used for go behinds on the mat.   Practically the same counters apply in both cases.   Even though wrestler A does not intend to wrestle down on the mat face to face with his opponent, he should learn how to meet this situation because the natural course of the match may lead to it.   If he is well-versed in this phase of wrestling he will be better prepared to take care of himself.

COUNTERS TO THE DOUBLE ARM DRAG

CROSS-OVER

1. As wrestler B drags past A's right arm, A shifts all his weight to his left foot.
2. Throws his right leg up and across B's body, followed by his left leg.
3. His body should be perpendicular to B's and A's feet well spread.   A can now pin him with a crotch and half nelson.

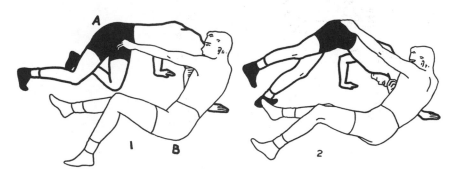

COUNTER DRAG

1. As his opponent drags past his right arm, A catches B's right arm just below the arm pit.   Shifts all his weight to his right foot.
2. Jerks B's right arm to his right and gets ready to set his left leg through.
3. A keeps pulling B past him to his right and sets his left leg through.
4. Pulls B forward to the mat.   A keeps B's right leg hooked with A's left leg so B cannot cross-over.   Uses his left arm to reach around B's waist.
5. Swings wide and comes on top to ride B.

COUNTER TO SHORT ARM DRAG

CROSS-OVER

1. A is tied up in referee's position head to head down on the mat.
2. When B short arm drags A to B's right, A shifts all his weight to his left foot.
3. Swings his right leg backward and across B's left leg.
4. A brings his arm back, placing right arm around B's waist and proceeds to ride him.

COUNTER TO HEAD DRAG

NEAR WING AND CROSS-OVER

1. As B sets through under A's right arm, A prepares to bring his own right arm down.
2. He locks his right arm around B's right arm and jerks B backward to the mat.
3. Shifts all his weight to his left foot and throws his right leg high over B's body followed by his left leg.
4. A should now be perpendicular to B's body with legs spread for good balance.

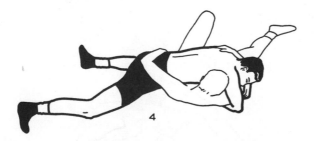

COUNTER TO SLAP DOWN

ARM HOOK

1. Wrestler B catches A's right arm just above the elbow where A cannot grasp B's neck to keep his balance.
2. A takes his left hand off B's right elbow and hooks it into the pit of B's right elbow. A can now prevent the slap down because when B snaps A's head down A also pulls B down so he cannot jump behind.

counters for take downs from behind

When wrestler B is behind him, A keeps good balance by keeping his own legs spread and his weight well distributed so he can shift quickly to counter any move B may make. The same counter may be used against many of the take downs from behind. This makes it less complicated to counter B's moves.

COUNTER FOR CROSS-OVER

SWITCH

1. As B crosses his legs over and drops to his right knee, A prepares to put his left hand into B's crotch.
2. A comes to the mat with his left arm over B's left arm ready to put on pressure.
3. A grasps B's left wrist with his right hand so B cannot pull his arm out. Puts pressure on B's left arm pit and A swings his buttock wide.
4. Turns and comes on top of B with his right arm around B's waist and his right leg astraddle B's left leg.

COUNTERS TO BACK HEEL

SWITCH

1. As B back heels him, A throws his left arm back to get ready to place it in B's crotch.
2. Note that A has pulled B to one side with his left hand in B's crotch and his right hand hold of B's left wrist.
3. A swings wide and comes on top as shown in illustration.

COUNTERS TO BACK HEEL: SWITCH

COUNTER TO OUTSIDE LEG TRIP

SWITCH

1. As B hooks his right leg over A's right leg to trip him forward, A gets his right arm ready.
2. As B brings A to the mat, A throws his right arm back toward B's crotch. At the same time A shifts all his weight to his right foot.
3. A pivots to his right on his right foot and sets his left leg through, at the same time, throws his right hand in B's crotch.
4. Swings wide and with his left hand reaches for a rear crotch and gets more leverage. Keeps left leg ready in case B tries a cross-over.
5. Swings out and comes on top as shown in illustration.

COUNTER TO OUTSIDE LEG TRIP: SWITCH

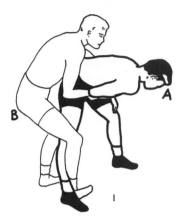

COUNTER FOR CROTCH PICK-UP

LEG HOOK AND DRAG

1. As B reaches for a crotch pick-up, A shifts all his weight to his left foot.
2. As B starts to pick up A's right leg, A hooks B's right leg with it as shown. At the same time A catches B's right elbow with his right hand.
3. As A comes to the mat, he raises B's right leg up with his right foot to keep B off balance.
4. A shifts his right hand to a drag position on B's right arm just below arm pit. He must be sure to keep B off balance with his right foot.
5. A jerks B to his right and swings wide and comes on top as shown in illustration.

COUNTER FOR CROTCH PICK UP: LEG HOOK AND DRAG

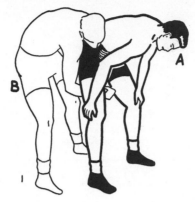

counters for reverses and escapes

A wrestler must know all the counters to the common methods of reverses and escapes if he is to be an exceptionally good rider. In many cases it is hard to distinguish where riding stops and counters begin. Some coaches refer to these counters as a part of break downs and rides.

It will be impossible to keep a tough opponent broken down at all times and that is why it is imperative that considerable time should be spent in working on these most common counters. As long as his adversary can keep on all fours he is dangerous and can force A to rely on these counters to keep his position of advantage.

To be a good rider, a wrestler must have a thorough knowledge of chain wrestling. His opponent will force him to use this position if A is not able to control. B may lure A into one position in order to set him up for another and if A is not well versed in the maneuver he can lose his opponent. This is why a novice cannot hope to cope with a clever wrestler.

The best counter is to keep B off balance and broken down into a prone position where he is unable to work reverses and escapes. In other words keep B busy trying to get out of rides and break downs. A must not shoot all his own energy. He must control his opponent and force B to burn up his energy.

COUNTER TO SWITCHES

NEAR ARM TIE UP

1. As his opponent pivots out to switch, A catches B's near arm with his hand. as shown.
2. Breaks B's arm out from under him at the same time A throws his left shoulder and left arm into B, forcing him down on his right side. A will now have B in a very good position to ride.

CROSS-OVER

1. When B pivots out in a position where he is sitting on his buttock, A shifts all his weight to his right foot.
2. Then throws his left leg up and across B's body followed by his right leg.
3. A should now be in a perpendicular position to B's body with feet well spread.

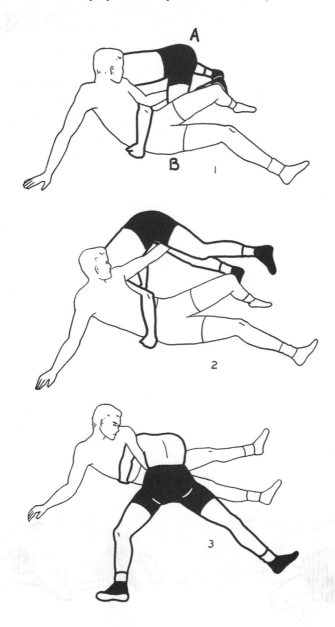

COUNTER SWITCH

1. When B pivots out in a position where he is sitting on his buttock, A keeps his left knee against B's left hip. At the same time A shifts all his weight to his left foot and right hand.
2. As B turns to come on top A applies the same pressure to B's left arm by prying up on it. Keeps his left knee against B's hip and off the mat. Starts his pivot on left foot.
3. A sets his right leg through and puts pressure on B's left shoulder. All A's weight is on his own left foot and right hand.
4. He is now sitting on his buttock. A puts the pressure on him and swings away from him. A is now trying to keep B from re-countering his counter switch.
5. If A can put enough leverage on B's left shoulder to force it to the mat and then swing his own buttock away from B, he can get control of B.
6. Swing wide and come on top as shown.

COUNTER TO SWITCHES: COUNTER SWITCH

COUNTERS TO WINGLOCKS

FLATTEN OUT

1. As B grasps his left hand on A's left wrist, A shifts his weight away from B.
2. When B starts his roll, A shifts his weight back and shoves on B's right elbow in order to keep his own weight well distributed.   He must be sure to keep his left leg hooked over B's right leg.
3. By now A should have countered B's roll as shown in this illustration.

CROSS-OVER

1. As B grasps his right hand on A's right wrist, A shifts all his weight to his left foot.
2. When B rolls by dropping down on his right side, A starts his cross-over by springing off his left foot.   At the same time B may kick A's left leg high but A keeps his balance by spreading his legs.
3. As B keeps on rolling, A notes that B's left leg finally comes to the mat. This will give him the opportunity to get his own leg off B's and comes into a perpendicular position as shown in this illustration.

CROSS BODY RIDE

1. As B grasps his right hand on A's right wrist, A keeps B's left leg hooked with A's right leg.   This counter can be used as a last resort when the other two fail.
2. As B rolls and kicks A's left leg up, A keeps his right foot on the mat and spread for balance.
3. Slides his left leg up and over B's knee.
4. Brings his left arm up and over B's right shoulder and hooks it around B's right arm pit.   At the same time A hooks his left leg around B's left leg.
5. A gets his right hand free and grasps B's right wrist.   Uses both legs on B's left foot.

COUNTERS TO WINGLOCKS: CROSS BODY RIDE

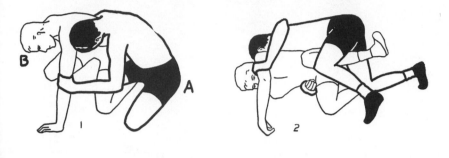

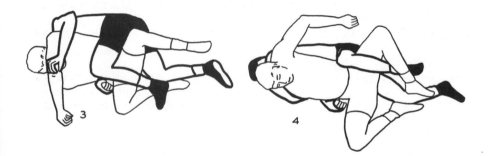

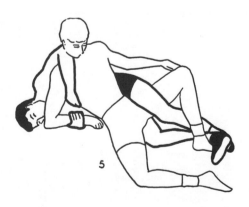

COUNTERS TO SET-OUTS

NEAR ARM TIE UP

1. A starts from the referee's position.
2. As B brings up his right foot, A slides his left hand down on B's left wrist.
3. As B throws his left leg through, A pulls B's left arm back.
4. Drives his own right shoulder and arm into B and breaks B down on his left side as shown in this illustration.

COUNTERS TO SET OUTS: NEAR ARM TIE UP

ARM LOCK AND CHIN COUNTER

1. As B brings his right foot up A shifts his right hand up under B's right arm pit.
2. As B throws his left leg through, A hooks his left hand up through under B's left arm pit.
3. A pulls B back toward A to keep him off balance.
4. While B is off balance, A throws his left arm up and over B's left arm and hooks it just above the elbow.
5. A shoves B to A's right so he can get his head on top of B's left shoulder and at the same time A can move his left arm up under B's left arm pit.
6. Wrestler A takes his right arm out from under B's right arm pit and grasps his around and under the chin.
7. Snaps B back on his shoulders and holds him there.

COUNTERS TO SET OUTS: ARM LOCK AND CHIN COUNTER

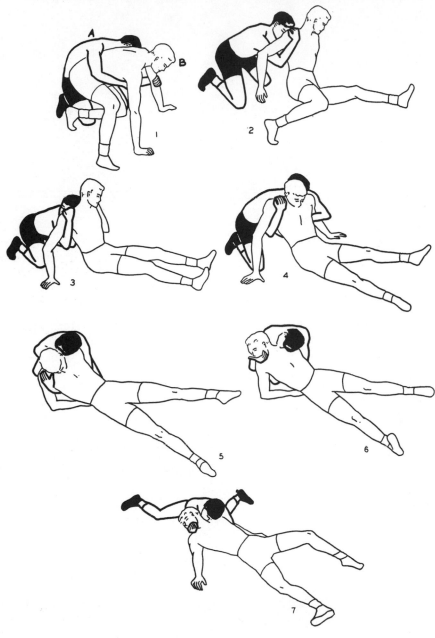

OVER DRAG

1. As B brings up his right foot, A gets ready to move his right hand up.
2. A grasps B under the right arm just below the shoulder as B sets his left leg through.
3. As B pivots on his left knee and left elbow, A holds on to B's right hand as shown.   Gets ready to spring behind B.
4. A pulls B's right arm forward and down, springing behind him.
5. He should land in about this position, as shown in the diagram to get ready to break him down.

COUNTERS TO SET OUTS: OVER DRAG

COUNTERS FOR STANDING POSITION

SET BACK

1. As his opponent comes up to both feet and still has both hands on mat, A shifts all his weight to left foot and knee.
2. Brings up right leg and hooks it around B's left leg. At the same time drops his shoulders down and under B.
3. As B stands up A shoots his left arm through and behind B's right leg as shown. At the same time thrusts his head and right shoulder into B. He must be sure he has pivoted around to B's front.
4. A drives B back with his head, shoulder and left arm. A is now ready to shift to an inside crotch ride.

LEG PICK UP

1. As B jumps to both feet, A shifts his right knee back to about middle distance between both feet, at the same time hooking left arm behind opponent's left knee.   A brings up his left foot for balance as shown in this illustration.
2. A times this move so that he picks up B's left leg with his left arm as B raises his hands from the mat.
3. As B keeps coming up to a standing position, A picks B's left leg up and turns B back across A's right arm.   A pivots on his right knee and brings his left leg on around.
4. A will now be in a position to assume an inside crotch ride as shown in illustration.

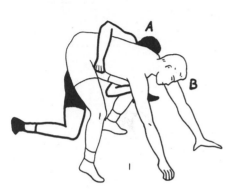

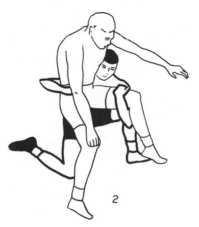

COUNTERS FOR HIP LOCKS

ARM ACROSS BUTTOCK

1. When his opponent hooks his left arm over A's right arm in hip lock position, A must be sure he keeps B's left leg hooked with his own right leg and keeps his knees well spread.
2. A quickly brings his right arm back across B's buttocks.
3. Jerks it forward hard and fast.
4. Then throws the arm back quickly and grasps B around the waist.

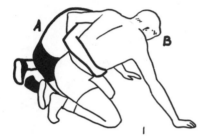

ARM PRY

1. When his opponent hooks his left arm over A's right arm in hip lock position A must keep B's left leg hooked with his own right leg and keep his knees well spread for good balance.
2. A brings his right arm forward quickly and grasps his left hand.
3. A pries B's arm down and forward, putting a lot of pressure on it.
4. This will force B's arm off A's arm as shown in this illustration.
5. As soon as A has accomplished this move, he brings his right arm back and places it around B's waist.

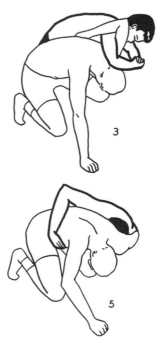

DOUBLE DOUBLE

1. When wrestler B hooks his left arm over A's right arm in a hip lock position A must be sure he keeps B's left leg hooked by his own right leg and keeps his knees spread for good balance.
2. Immediately A throws his left arm over B's neck.
3. Locks his hands together, putting pressure on B's neck and forcing it into the mat.
4. This should put B's shoulders on the mat.   A must be sure to bring B's left leg toward his so B's head will be between B's legs.   A shifts all his weight back on B's left leg to get better balance.

counters for pin holds

A wrestler may be exceptionally good on take downs and rides and still lose a match unless he can set up a good defense against the common methods of riding and pinning combinations.

There are four stages in preparing a defense against pin holds. First, he must be able to defend himself against the common methods of break downs and rides. It is almost impossible for a wrestler to pin an opponent unless he is able to break him down and ride him. There are exceptional cases where a wrestler has fallen into a pinning combination but this is unusual.

The second stage is to learn and develop the fundamental counters against half nelsons. Once this has been accomplished it is almost impossible to get pinned.

Once wrestler A's defense against the first two stages has failed and B has him in a pinning combination on his side, A is ready to start his third phase of defense. Keeping himself in a good position, he drops on his hip first. He keeps his elbow under him so when B applies more pressure on A's neck A's shoulder will not go to the mat but he will be able to rise up on the elbow. While B is applying the pressure, A resists with everything he has. This is merely setting B up; all of a sudden A goes with him. Having his elbow on the mat will bring A's shoulders up and he can shove B's pressure and weight toward his own hip. A can throw his feet out from under him and come on top. This move will be demonstrated in some of the illustrations shown in this chapter.

The last stage in A's defense is when B has his shoulders near the mat. A wrestler should learn a few counters in this last phase. We will discuss only those counters that apply to the pin holds treated in a previous chapter.

COUNTER TO BAR ARM AND HALF NELSON

SIDE OUT

1. When wrestler B starts a half nelson, A keeps his head up.
2. Brings his left leg up to his left to brace himself and throws his head back.

ELBOW ROLL

1. This is the beginning of the third stage of defense as discussed in the introduction of this chapter.   Note he should drop on left hip and keep his elbow on mat.
2. A catches B's right arm with his right hand as shown in illustration.   He hooks his right foot just above B's left knee.
3. Rolls, kicks B's left leg, with his right hand A pulls up and down on B's right arm.   Note he is on his elbow and in a position where he has the advantage of leverage on B.
4. Turns and comes on top as shown in illustration.   Keeps feet spread to keep balance and power.

COUNTER TO BAR ARM AND HALF NELSON: SIDE OUT

COUNTER TO BAR ARM AND HALF NELSON: ELBOW ROLL

COUNTERS TO CROTCH AND HALF NELSON

BRIDGE UP

1. A is now in the fourth and final stage of a defense, again a pin hold. Brings his right arm up and places it under B's chest. At the same time A tries to keep his right shoulder off the mat.
2. A bridges up and B's chest will be tight against his. Both feet should be well up under A and spread.
3. Then A comes back to the mat quickly. This will leave a little space between their two chests. As A moves his chest away from B, he shoves his right arm between them as far as possible. A keeps his right shoulder off mat.
4. He bridges up again as far as possible.
5. Then comes back to the mat quickly leaving a gap between their two chests. Shoves his right arm completely through. He might have to repeat this operation again in order to get it completely through.
6. Now A turns on his stomach.
7. Gets up on knees and he will be in good shape to continue to wrestle.

COUNTERS TO CROTCH AND HALF NELSON: BRIDGE UP

ROLL OVER

1. B has A on his back. A tries to get B out of position by getting as near parallel to him as possible. A brings his right arm up at the same time. Puts his left arm between his legs and around his right leg.
2. A locks his two hands together.   Note right foot is ready to drive off.
3. He is now as near parallel as he can get.
4. Bridges up, starts his roll by pulling B's right leg up.
5. A turns and comes on top.   He has B in a crotch and half nelson. A must not make the same mistake B did by letting his opponent get parallel to him.

COUNTERS TO CROTCH AND HALF NELSON: ROLL OVER

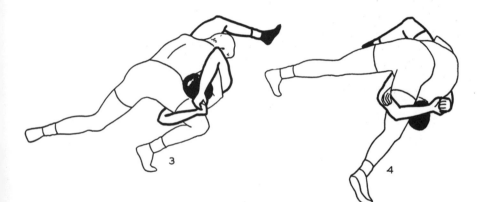

COUNTERS TO CHICKEN WING AND HALF NELSON

ELBOW ROLL

1. B is now in position to turn. A.   A concentrates on putting his elbow in the mat.
2. As B applies the pressure, A drops on right hip and stays up on elbow.
3. A catches B under the right arm pit with his left hand and pulls down.   Note A is rising up on elbow.
4. He turns and comes on top.   Kicks his feet free of B's feet.
5. Gets his legs perpendicular to B's body and well spread.

COUNTERS TO CHICKEN WING AND HALF NELSON: ELBOW ROLL

COUNTER DRAG

1. Note that in this illustration B is grasping A's right wrist with his left hand. When B gets ready to move his left hand for a half nelson, A gets ready to shift his weight to his right foot.
2. Immediately upon turning his wrist loose, A places his right hand back of B's right arm just above the elbow.   A keeps his head up in defense against half nelson.
3. A pivots on his right foot and pulls up and forward on B's right arm as shown.
4. Drags B forward and down.   Reaches for a rear crotch with the left hand. At the same time shifts all his weight to left foot.
5. He now has his opponent in a chicken wing and in a good riding position.

COUNTERS TO CHICKEN WING AND HALF NELSON: COUNTER DRAG

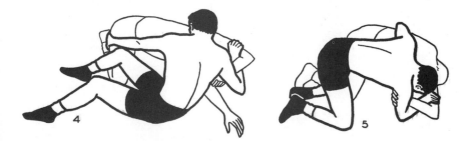

COUNTER TO ARM LOCK AND BODY PRESS

FLATTEN OUT

1. Note B has A flattened out on his stomach.   A keeps feet spread.
2. Brings his right leg up and places it as near a right angle as possible.   He is now in good position to resist B's pressure.

COUNTERS TO THREE QUARTER NELSON

HEAD UP

1. As B applies the three quarter nelson, A throws his head up so B cannot lock hands and put pressure on A's neck.

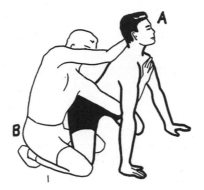

FLATTEN OUT

1. B now has A's neck in a three quarter nelson.
2. The only thing for A to do is to flatten out on his stomach so that his head cannot be turned under.

COUNTERS TO DOUBLE DOUBLE

HEAD UP

1. A has his right arm over B's left arm in a hip lock.
2. As B throws his right arm over A's neck to hook his left hand, A throws his head up and back.   B cannot lock hands to get leverage on A's neck.

HEAD DRAG

1. A has his right arm locked over B's left arm in a hip lock position.
2. As B throws his right arm over A's neck, A shifts all his weight to his right foot and left hand.   Raises his right knee off the mat and gets ready to pivot.
3. A throws his head back and sets his left leg through.
4. Pivots wide and shifts all his weight on left foot.   Places his left arm up and around B's back.
5. A cuts his right leg back under his left leg, keeping them spread and his body perpendicular to B's as shown in diagram.

COUNTERS TO DOUBLE DOUBLE: HEAD DRAG

grips, counters for half nelsons, arm and leg holds

It is imperative that wrestlers know all the grips and counters for half nelsons, arm and leg holds. The average wrestler may feel that these counters are so simple that they do not mean much. But he must remember that once his arms and legs get tied up in a hard match he must get free or the match is lost. He can get pinned because he doesn't know a simple counter to a half nelson. Then he will realize how important it is to practice these simple fundamentals. He will probably have the opportunity to use these counters more than any other moves in wrestling.

The illustrations in this chapter will deal with the most common grips, counters to half nelsons, arm and leg holds.

THE MOST COMMON GRIPS

HOOK GRIP

1. Wrestler A holds his fingers in the form of a hook as shown in this illustration.
2. Then he hooks his fingers together and turns his thumb in to protect it when falling to mat.

CUP GRIP

1. He forms his hand in the shape of a cup by bending fingers and thumb at right angle. Keeps one hand with palm down and turns the other at a right angle.
2. Locks his thumb and fingers together in the shape of a cup.

INTER-LACE GRIP

1. He bends his fingers at a right angle. Spreads his index and second finger; spreads his little and third finger. Note that his thumb is getting ready to go between these openings.
2. Then he locks his thumb between the little and third finger. At the same time his index finger locks between the little and third finger. This is the strongest grip but it takes more time to get it.

THE MOST COMMON GRIPS: HOOK GRIP

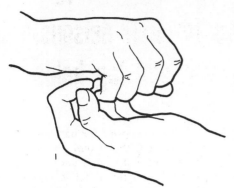
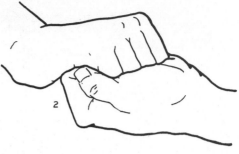

THE MOST COMMON GRIPS: CUP GRIP

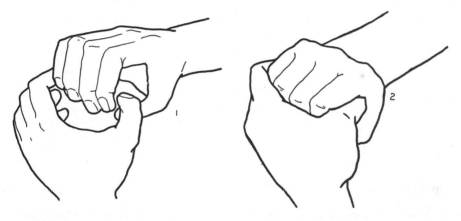

THE MOST COMMON GRIPS: INTER-LACE GRIP

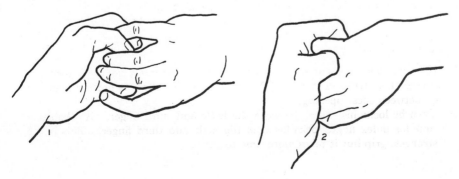

COUNTERS TO SINGLE ARM HOLDS

KNOCK HAND OFF

1. In order to free his right arm, wrestler A brings his left hand across to hit wrestler B's four fingers with the heel of the hand.
2. Note that A has knocked his opponent's right hand free of A's right arm. He must immediately make his move or B will regrasp it.

WRIST TWIST

1. As B uses a head lever to pry A's right arm back, A resists with everything he has.
2. Then all of a sudden, A goes with B, quickly turning his right hand up.
3. He brings his hand up and over the wrist of B's right arm.   This move takes advantage of simple leverage.
4. A's arm is now free but he must make a quick maneuver from here or he may loose his advantage.

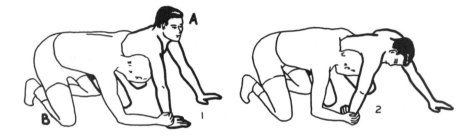

FOREARM TWIST

1. As B uses a head lever to pry A's left arm back, A resists with everything he has.   This is merely setting B up.
2. Then all of a sudden, A turns his left wrist in with palm of the hand up as shown in illustration.
3. Note also that he drops his left elbow to the mat.   His arm will be free.

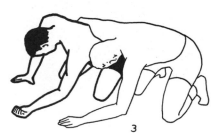

ARM TWIST

1. Wrestler B has A's right wrist tied up in a single bar arm with B's right hand.
2. A straightens his right arm out as shown.
3. Then throws his elbow back into B's forearm.
4. A turns his own forearm up and his arm will be free.

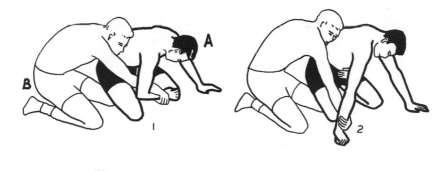

COUNTERS FOR DOUBLE BAR ARM

INTER-ARM COUNTER

1. Wrestler B is behind A and both his hands grip around A's right wrist.
2. A puts his left arm under B's left forearm.   Grasps B's right wrist with his left hand.
3. A then pries up on B's left forearm with his left forearm, shoving down on B's right wrist with his left hand.   At the same time, A turns his right wrist down and pries up with right forearm.   The timing is important, it must be a quick, smooth operation.
4. Note that A has shoved his hands straight down and his arms should be free. This is a clever use of leverages.

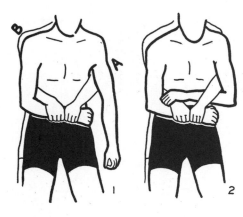

PULL HAND OFF AND ARM TWIST

1. Wrestler B is behind A and both his hands grip around A's right wrist.
2. With his left hand, A grasps all four fingers of B's left hand.
3. Then pulls them off his right wrist.
4. A holds on to B's left hand by the fingers.   At the same time A straightens out his right arm.
5. Then he throws his right elbow back into B's right forearm, and turns the wrist up to get leverage.   He is now free to make his next move.

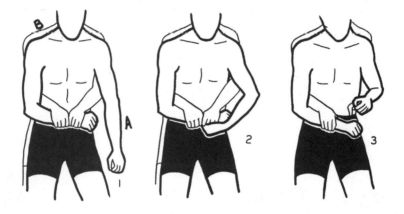

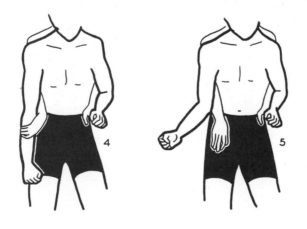

COUNTERS FOR LEG HOLDS

INSIDE LEG HOLD

1. The opponent reaches back between his legs to grasp A's right leg.
2. As he pulls it toward him, A hooks it behind B's right ankle. B is pulling against his own leg; A has blocked the move.

OUTSIDE LEG HOLD

1. Wrestler B reaches back to the outside of his right leg and grasps A's right ankle with both his hands.
2. A lets B bring A's foot forward, and hooks it behind B's right foot. B is now pulling against his own leg; A has countered his move.

GRAPEVINE LEG

1. When A's opponent is behind him and has his hands locked around A's waist, often B will try to pick A up and take him to the mat. The best way to counter this move is for A to hook his right foot behind B's right ankle. When B picks him up, B is merely pulling against his own leg. A must be sure to keep his left leg spread from the other to give him a good base.

COUNTERS FOR LEG HOLDS: INSIDE LEG HOLD

COUNTERS FOR LEG HOLDS: OUTSIDE LEG HOLD

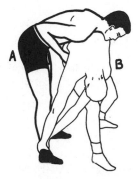

COUNTERS FOR LEG HOLDS: GRAPEVINE LEG

COUNTERS FOR HALF NELSONS

PULL HAND OFF

1. Opponent has a half nelson on A's neck.
2. A reaches up with his left hand and grasps B's left hand.
3. Pulls B's left off his neck and turns his head away.

TURN HEAD AWAY AND UP

1. Opponent has a half nelson on A's neck.
2. A locks his left arm around B's left arm just above the elbow.   A jerks down on the elbow and turns his head up.

SIDE OUT

1. Opponent has a half nelson on A's neck.
2. A slides his leg out to his right.
3. He is now in almost a set-out position to his right.   He locks his left arm around B's left arm.

NEAR WING AND CROSS-OVER

1. Opponent has half nelson on the side next to him.
2. A locks his left arm around B's left arm just above the elbow.
3. Jerks B's left arm down and into the mat and then A throws his left leg up high.
4. He crosses over B's body with both legs.
5. A should come across B's body as shown.

NEAR UNDER ARM DRAG

1. Opponent has half nelson on A on the side next to him.
2. A takes his left hand and grasps B's left arm just above the elbow.   B is straddling A's left leg.
3. A shifts all his weight to the left foot and right hand.   Raises his left knee off mat and at the same time, pulls up on B's left arm.
4. Pivots on his left foot and throws his right leg through, pulling down on B's left arm.
5. A keeps pulling down on B's left arm and reaches around B's waist with his right arm.   A keeps his right leg in position to block cross-over.   Then he turns and comes on top.

FAR WING

1. Opponent has half nelson on A's neck from the far side.
2. A locks his right arm around B's right arm just above the elbow.
3. Jerks down on B's right arm and A starts to roll on his right hip.
4. Then throws his feet away from B in a perpendicular position.
5. Then A turns toward B's feet and comes on top of him in the position as shown in illustration.

COUNTERS FOR HALF NELSONS: FAR WING

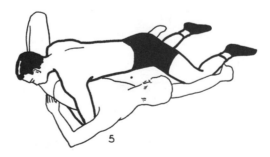

FARTHER UNDER ARM DRAG

1. Opponent has half nelson on A's neck from the far side.
2. With his right hand A catches B just at the right elbow.
3. He shifts all his weight to the right foot and left hand. Raises right knee off mat, at the same time, pulls up on B's right elbow.
4. Then A pivots on his right foot by bringing his left leg through. At the same time, A jerks down on B's right elbow.
5. A pulls down on B's right arm. Reaches across with his left arm and puts it around B's waist.
6. A comes on top as shown in illustration.

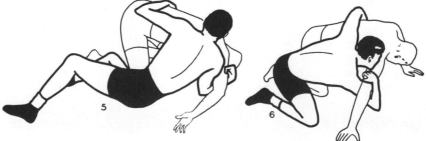

chapter 19

methods in teaching wrestling classes

The methods which the instructor uses will depend a great deal upon his personality. An instructor will be successful in proportion to his ability to keep young in spirit and to keep before him the interests and desires of the young men he has to teach. Many instructors, after spending several years in the profession, harden and lose the perspective of their younger days. To know young people and to live with them on their own level is a tremendously effective instrument in molding their minds and abilities. He must be able to command their respect on and off the mat.

The wrestling instructor must learn to spend his time economically in order to get the full value of skills out of every practice period. This is merely applying sound principles of business management.

The Instructor

The instructor must realize that he is more than just a teacher. He builds character, molds personalities, and exerts a profound influence on the life of youngsters at a very formative period of their lives.

An instructor must be fair and honorable to his squad. To watch a squad work is to know the teacher for their work reflects the personality and attitudes of the coach.

The enthusiasm he generates will be an inspiration to his men and the class will reflect this in their actions. An instructor must remember that while he teaches one class after another and it may become monotonous to him, it is a new, fresh experience to each class of wrestlers. He should recognize that merely giving technical instruction in the skills of wrestling is not enough; he must be dynamic and forceful as well.

Patience cannot be overemphasized when teaching beginners in wrestling as it is so easy for them to become discouraged. In teaching a new skill it is important that the directions be given clearly and understood thoroughly. Refrain from haranguing and embarrassing your class. A lack of patience on the part of the instructor will seriously affect the progress of a wrestler.

The instructor at all times must be ready to give words of praise and encouragement when merited; at the same time he must be a strict disciplinarian. No instructor can be successful if he does not have control over his class. He must meet the first encounter with determination and come off winner.

He must have confidence in his own ability to teach wrestling. If he believes and acts as though he expects the class to respond according to his wishes, they will do it. He should always have something to offer the class which will improve them and at the same time he must be alert to new ideas. No matter how long he has been teaching wrestling he can pick up some new ideas from the poorest member of his class. He must have confidence in his ability as a teacher.

A sense of humor is a great asset in teaching wrestling. It will carry the instructor through many difficulties. He can take advantage of any humorous situation that might happen in class to relieve the tension and relax the boys. However, he must be able to get his class back under control.

A wrestling instructor needs to acquire a commanding voice and to learn to speak with authority. Shouting is not necessary, for he needs to be patient when working with a group. A friendly atmosphere is essential for a class cannot learn as rapidly under pressure.

Instructors of wrestling must develop an imagination, for many of the moves are complicated and need quick thinking. If one method of teaching does not work he must be quick to seize on one that he has not tried before. There are many different approaches in teaching the same skill. He must not get into a rut; if his most popular method fails, he should try a new one.

A wrestling instructor must know the skills of wrestling, the leverages used and how to apply them. He must know the strong and weak points of every maneuver; what the opponent can do to counter and how the wrestler may offset this counter. If he does not have this knowledge he may lead his men into a trap or get them lost in a maze of maneuvers. He must be a student of wrestling and know all the phases of the sport. He should study the various parts of a skill from all angles and analyze the ones that will be hard to put across before teaching it.

In order to teach efficiently, it is absolutely necessary to have a carefully prepared lesson plan. A conscientious instructor will always have one. He must know the number of class periods and the length of time for each. With this information he can prepare a teaching schedule for the entire season. After deciding what is to be taught, the good instructor will have a definite teaching progression with one step leading directly to the next step in a logical order.

Every minute of a class period must be utilized to the fullest extent. The ability to organize is extremely important. The best instructor will keep a class on the move for the entire session. He must be quick to recognize fatigue and shift from the strenuous work to the type that will give them a chance to recuperate, such as drills, demonstration of holds and maneuvers. Coaching is a fight against time and every minute must count.

To make teaching more effective, he must have the ability to demonstrate what he is teaching. It is not necessary that he be an expert, but he should be able to do the skills fairly well. When demonstrating moves, he should do them slowly enough so that all wrestlers will be able to see the important steps involved. Each skill should be demonstrated several times to emphasize each important phase of the maneuver.   He must acquire the ability to speak well while demonstrating.

Wrestling can get complicated, so it is easy for a student to make faulty moves.   The instructor must have the ability to arrest the motion in his own thinking so he will know exactly what the student is doing wrong.   Correcting mistakes is one of the most important phases of successful teaching.   To tell the wrestler about the faulty moves is not enough.   He must be able to offer constructive criticism and to do it in such a way that the student will be at ease.

The wrestling instructor must have an educational background and should know the philosophy and aims of general education and physical education. He should be well versed in hygiene, physiology, psychology, anatomy, and sociology.   It is important that he know the interests and characteristics of each age level.   He should always place the welfare of his wrestlers above his own personal ambitions.   A high standard of ethics must be maintained as well as a complete technical knowledge of the sport.

Methods in Teaching Wrestling

There are a number of conditions and factors which will affect the learning of a class.   It is up to the instructor to be alert to these conditions and to alter his practice to meet these situations in order to get the most out of his class.   The prerequisite of any instructor who wants to make the most out of his coaching is to have his program well outlined before he meets the student at the mat.

Giving instructions to a class is quite different from developing a wrestling team for competition.   In a wrestling class it is necessary that he present his material in a formal manner and more or less in the nature of drills.   He is not primarily concerned in developing an individual but in teaching the fundamentals to the entire class.   While on the other hand in developing a wrestling team for competition he is more concerned with individuals and particularly those few individuals of outstanding abilities.

For an instructor to get the most out of a wrestling season it is better to have a greater number of practice periods of lesser length than fewer periods of greater length.   Occasionally an instructor fails to adhere to these laws of learning and as a result the beginner wrestler becomes lost in a mass of maneuvers.   It is better to teach a few fundamentals and have them well developed than to show the class the book and have them confused.   The old saying that "practice makes perfect" is correct if the instructor uses good common sense in the economy of time.   For example, it is foolish to practice any one given skill beyond a reasonable time without adequate rest.   It leads to ineffective repetitions.

At the beginning of the season it may be advantageous to practice twice daily on skills, but after a few practices, once a day is sufficient.   Near the end of the wrestling season it is better to work on certain skills only every other day.

Many of the maneuvers in wrestling are complicated and in teaching beginners, learning is most effective when the whole-part-whole method is used.   First, the instructor should demonstrate the complete maneuver.   Then he should divide it into parts.   The class should master each part separately and then combine the parts together as a unit. The instructor should then go back and demonstrate the complete maneuver once more, in order that the class gets a complete picture of the hold. This will prevent bad habits which the beginner may develop and later will have to undo.

The emotional state of a wrestler is important. Fear and anger may cause a beginner to be unable to relax and to overstrain his muscles. This is particularly true among beginners who have a tendency to use too much strength and have not learned to relax.

The number of skills in wrestling one learns will depend upon experience, ability, interest, and desire. Instructors have a tendency toward trying to develop too many maneuvers and as a result they sacrifice proficiency. It is better to concentrate on mastering the fundamentals of wrestling. It is the perfection in fundamentals that distinguishes the champions in all sports. It is better to arrange that a cross-section of the sport be presented each day. The coach should not spend the entire period on one area of the sport; such as takedowns, escapes, reverses, or any other particular phase of wrestling. He should have his lesson plan worked out so something new can be presented from two or three areas each day. The group will get a more comprehensive idea of the objectives of wrestling and a better conception of the sport. They will also have a better understanding of how to correlate one maneuver into another stage.

The rate of learning depends upon the way the material is organized and presented. The coach must consider the type of individual he has, as no two students are alike in their response to the course. The abilities of individuals are different; some are strong, others are slow, while others are quick and react fast. There is a difference in builds; the tall, short, and medium, hence they cannot all work the same type of holds effectively. The instructor must study the individual, try out various maneuvers, and fit those that come most naturally to the wrestler who is to use them. Some will be strong on certain types of holds such as takedowns, while others will be weak on the same group. However, every member of a wrestling team should know the important holds even though he cannot work all of them. He must be prepared to counter when he comes in contact with the various maneuvers.

Every minute of a practice period must be utilized. The wrestler must be attentive if he is to learn, but he finds it difficult to hold his attention when he is fatigued. His reflexes are slower, his timing is off, and he is beginning to lose his sense of balance. It is better to give frequent rest periods. This doesn't mean that the class should lie around and rest, but that the coach take advantage of these breaks to demonstrate new maneuvers or emphasize old ones, or discuss other phases of the sport.

Class Details

There are several methods of conducting a wrestling class. However, there are certain fundamental patterns in class organization that the best instructors use. Divide the class into two groups, calling them one and two. Each member of group one should be assigned a partner of corresponding weight from group two. Have the class form a circle on the mat large enough to allow plenty of room for the demonstrations and then have them sit down.

Use one of the best students to demonstrate the hold. The demonstration should be given before a maneuver is attempted by the class and should be repeated several times. The analysis of the skill should be presented very slowly. An ideal demonstrator is one who dissects and reassembles the maneuver with clear continuity.* The common faults and errors should be pointed out and explained. Also the situations where this particular hold would be most applicable should be called to their attention.

One group should be called upon to execute the maneuver against their partners on the command of the instructor. Each step of the hold should be announced by the instructor. Have the entire group go through the maneuver in unison, step by step on the command of the instructor. Then reverse the procedure and have the other group do the same thing. The most complicated maneuvers should be dissected and each part done separately, then reassembled and done all together. After it has been executed several times, the hold should be demonstrated again, with the instructor pointing out their common faults and errors. The class should then be called upon to repeat the drill emphasizing the most common mistakes. After the corrections have been made, have them move at a faster tempo.

When the class begins to catch on to the hold, shorten the commands or even have them do it by numbers as each hold can usually be dissected into four or five steps. The instructor can judge the tempo according to the way the class is responding.

It is hard to get a group to offer the right amount of resistance. The group on defense must react to the situation normally and try to resist to the extent necessary for the offensive wrestler to get the "feel" of the hold. They should apply enough pressure to the offensive wrestler so he can get the timing and learn how to apply the greatest amount of leverage.

Never show the counter to any hold until the student can execute the maneuver with some degree of success. When he has accomplished this, then show him the counter. This is also true in showing the counter to the counter which leads into "chain wrestling." If the wrestler is not allowed to get in advance of the counter he will lose confidence in his ability to use that particular maneuver.

The first prerequisite of a good instructor is to get his class warmed up well and then review the previous day's assignments. This should be followed with demonstrations of some new holds. This will keep the class interested and alert.

Class Control

To teach efficiently it is best to require that all members of the group perform the same operation together. The best way to accomplish this is to have all maneuvers start and stop with the sound of a whistle. The whistle should speak with authority and the class must be made to understand this. Some members will be inclined to continue with their wrestling after the whistle blows, but this wastes time and cannot be tolerated.

---

*See John A. Torney, Jr., *Swimming*, 1st. Ed., New York: McGraw-Hill, 1950, p. 70.

The First Day

On the first day the instructor should spend some time in explaining the general purpose and objectives of wrestling, the high-lights of the rules, and the regulations of conduct and procedure he intends to maintain in class.

The instructor should take time in demonstrating the warm-up drills and at the same time explain how they fit in with wrestling.

All illegal and dangerous holds should be demonstrated in this first period, each group should go through these holds. It is important that the student is able to realize when he has an opponent in a dangerous position. This knowledge will keep injuries to a minimum.

The instructor is now ready to teach the fundamental positions and moves, such as stance, the position of the feet, and footwork. The first area of wrestling that should be taught is "take downs." This is the offense of wrestling and the hardest to teach.

The Wrestling Areas

Wrestling can be taught better when divided into several areas. All holds should be divided into these areas.

1. *Take downs*
2. *Go behind on the mat*
3. *Take downs from behind*
4. *Riding and break downs*
5. *Reverses and escapes*
6. *Pinning holds*
7. *Counters to all important holds*

To be a good wrestler one must be proficient in all these areas. It is not enough just to know the holds; he must develop the counters and blocks, and know where the holds lead. Wrestlers must realize that all holds can be countered, especially when meeting an opponent of equal ability. Every feint or fake should be made for the purpose of setting an opponent up for one which is to follow. When one position is countered the opponent is usually open for a move from another angle.

Working the Class

In teaching a wrestling class the instructor should not make a lecture course out of it, nor should it be a drill period for holds. The student will learn more in ten minutes of wrestling than can be explained to him in an hour of lecture or drills. After the student has learned the holds through demonstrations and drills he must put it to use under competitive conditions and against several different opponents. They should get plenty of this type of work. The length of time they work will depend on their condition. Have a large mat area so the entire class can be working. Don't have one match going and the rest of the class sitting around looking on.

Have the entire class work on one area at a time such as take downs. This will keep injuries to a minimum as it will prevent one pair falling over the others. Just as soon as they score take downs have them get back on their feet and wrestle for take downs again.   There is one exception to this and that is when a wrestler has his opponent in a pinning combination.   They keep on working until he is pinned or his opponent gets out of the hold.   This teaches the wrestlers to take advantage of openings and at the same time teaches the one on defense to cover up.

The Warm-up Period

At the beginning of each class about five minutes should be devoted to warm-up exercises.   There are six fundamental qualities which are essential in developing fitness for wrestling.   These are speed, strength, flexibility, agility, endurance, and balance.   Many of the moves in wrestling may be used profitably in warming up.   Particularly those routines which develop definite wrestling maneuvers, such as switching, setting out, and bridging.   The following exercises have been selected to develop these necessary qualities.

1. *Cross-over—starting position, feet apart, hands on hips.*
    (a) Bring the right hand across and touch the left ankle.
    (b) Return to starting position.
    (c) Bring the left hand across and touch right ankle.
    (d) Return to starting position.

2. *Combining knee bends with back bends—starting position, feet together, arms to a thrust.*
    (a) Come to a full squat and thrust arms forward.
    (b) Return to a starting position.
    (c) Bend forward and touch toes, legs straight.
    (d) Return to starting position.

3. *Stretching—starting position—feet apart, hook thumbs together, legs straight.*
    (a) Thrust head between legs as far back as possible, keeping legs straight.
    (b) Return to starting position, dragging back of hands on mat.

4. *Bridging (front and back)—Supine lying.*
    (a) Arch back so feet and head are supporting points.   Work neck back and forward and then from side to side.   Then rotate neck keeping arms folded across chest.   Then turn to a front position and do the same except place hands just above the knees.

5. *Push-ups—starting position—assume a front leaning rest position, hands the width of shoulders apart, feet together, back straight.*
    (a) Bend elbows until chest touches mat.
    (b) Return to starting position.

6. *Sit-ups—starting position—lying flat on back, arms over head, feet together.*
    (a) Sit up, throwing arms forward touching toes with hands.
    (b) Return to starting position.

7. *Leg Cross-over—starting position—lying on back, arms sideward, feet together.*
    (a) Bring right foot across and touch left hand keeping back flat on mat.
    (b) Return to starting position.
    (c) Bring left foot across and touch right hand to mat.
    (d) Return to starting position.

8. *Switching—starting position—from referee's position on the mat, switching and counter switching. Don't let either one tie the other's arms up. Change sides so they can learn to switch from either side.*

9. *Sit-outs—starting position—from the referee's position on the mat—sit out and make a quick turn either way, at the same time have a top man counter with over-drag. Work from both sides.*

10. *Floating—starting position—the top man places all his weight by resting his chest on the underneath man's back. The underneath man tries to maneuver every possible way while the top man tries to keep his balance without losing his hold.*

Lesson Plan

The following is an example of how a class may be conducted on a basis of a forty-five minute period. If the period is shorter, then eliminate some of the material. If a longer period is available, then more practice can be given.

1. *Warm-up (5 minutes)*
    (a) Cross-over
    (b) Combine knee bends and back bends
    (c) Push-ups
    (d) Sit-ups
    (e) Leg cross-over
    (f) Bridging (front and back)
    (g) Stretching
    (h) Sit-outs

2. *Review (15 minutes)*
    (a) Double arm drag
    (b) Winglock
    (c) Crotch and half nelson

3. *New Holds (15 minutes) Demonstrations and drills*
    (a) Leg dive (demonstration)
    (b) Leg dive (drill)
       (1) Assume the closed stance position.
       (2) Duck head quickly and jerk his head forward.

       (3) Drop on both knees with head against opponent's side. Arms around legs.

       (4) Bring left leg forward and to outside.

       (5) Throw head back and to opponent's side and start pivoting on right knee.

       (6) Pivot around and move arms up around waist. Straddle opponent's right leg.

  (c) Repeat demonstration after two or three drills making corrections.

  (d) Repeat drills two or three times.

  (e) Switch (demonstration)

  (f) Switch (drill)

       (1) Opponent (wrestler B) is to wrestler A's left in referee's position.

       (2) With his right hand A knocks his opponent's left hand off his left arm.

       (3) A brings his left arm across to his right.

       (4) Shifts all his weight to his left hand and right foot, raising his knee off the mat at the same time.

       (5) Pivots his right foot and brings his left leg through to right. At the same time throws his right arm over B's right arm and into his crotch.

       (6) A leans back on B's right arm and swings his buttocks to the right.

       (7) Swings his buttock away from B to get more leverage and takes his left hand and reaches for a rear crotch.

       (8) Pulls B forward and comes on top.

  (g) Repeat demonstration of switch after two or three drills and make correction.

  (h) Repeat switch drill two or three times.

4. *Wrestle for take downs* (*5 minutes*)

5. *Wrestle down on mat* (*5 minutes*)

Grading Plan

    The character of any type of test must depend upon the purpose which it is to serve. Haphazard testing is a serious mistake and a waste of time. Wrestling instructors should limit the amount of testing in accordance to the length of time spent in the course. Tests should be set up so the majority of the class can pass with reasonable effort while a few will have to work hard to pass, and a few will fail. Standards should never be lowered in order to make a good showing. The tests that are used for grading should be simple, but comprehensive, and should be as objective as possible.

    The author has found through years of experience, that one of the best ways to grade students in a wrestling class is by performance test, written test and social attitudes.

Performance Test: The student is asked to wrestle a three two-minute period bout. While the bout is in progress the instructor grades them by areas on the different maneuvers they use. If all areas are not covered in the process of the bout, then the instructor will ask them to demonstrate some holds from the areas not covered in the match. In this way the instructor can evaluate what the student knows about the sport.

Written test: This is an objective type of test that covers the rules, strategy, and knowledge of the sport. Usually about forty questions are asked on this test, which makes it easy for the instructor to grade.

Social Attitudes: This covers the general attitudes of the student to his work in the class such as attendance, sportsmanship, healthmanship, etc.

The following is an example of the grading plan used:

Examination and Grading Plan

1. Performance Test—wrestling one six-minute match......... 60 points
   This test is given during the last three weeks of the quarter.
   Graded on the following basis:
   Take Downs...............................6 points
   Take Downs from behind....................6 points
   Reverses..................................6 points
   Escapes...................................6 points
   Rides.....................................6 points
   Pin Holds.................................6 points
   Take down counters.........................4 points
   Take down from behind counters.............4 points
   Reverse counters...........................4 points
   Escape counters............................4 points
   Pin hold counters..........................4 points
   Illegal holds..............................4 points
2. Written test—on rules, strategy, and knowledge of the sport,
   (40 questions, one-half point each)...................... 20 points
   This test is given the last week of the quarter.
3. Social attitudes—attendance, sportsmanship, healthmanship. 20 points

   TOTAL 100 points

methods of coaching varsity wrestling

Even though the varsity wrestling program provides direct benefits to only a limited number of selected wrestlers, it has a profound influence on the over-all program of wrestling. The techniques developed by the coaches are passed on through the instructional program in physical education and intramurals. Many a beginner and mediocre performer is inspired through observation and imitation of what the varsity wrestler does. From this he gets the desire to excel his fellow students. In those communities where wrestling has played a predominate part in sports there are many youths wrestling. The varsity program for these reasons profoundly affects wrestling in every phase and deserves a prominent place in the over-all program.

The First Squad Meeting

The first day that the coach assembles the wrestling squad he should give them the general outline and objectives of the program. He should emphasize the importance of keeping in superb physical condition during the season and explain that this can be accomplished only with patience and hard work. He should outline a carefully prepared training schedule and let them know that they are expected to carry it out. He should inform the squad of all regulations and rules of conduct which they are expected to observe.

The coach should emphasize the importance of a good warm-up period before each practice. Conditioning exercises and calisthenics should start on the first day and continue throughout the season. These exercises should use every part of the body. He must stress the importance of watching all demonstrations closely so that every detail of a maneuver can be followed.

He should continue to stress the importance of drills, for only through drills can wrestlers hope to master the maneuver. They must learn to put enough resistence in these drills to get the "feel of the hold" and develop good form.

Weight Class to Wrestle

It is an excellent idea for the wrestler and the coach to decide at the start of competition just which weight class each man expects to stay in for the season. The wrestler's welfare should be taken into consideration first of all. Excessive weight reduction is a vicious practice which sometimes causes wrestlers and the public to gain a distaste for the sport. This process of dehydration is the removal of body fluids from the three great tissues of the body, such as the heart, kidneys, and muscles.   If an excessive loss of weight is necessary it should be done under the advice of a competent medical authority.

High school wrestlers must realize that they will grow and gain weight during the season.   Other factors to be taken into consideration are: how one is built; slender, stocky, or fat.   A man of average size should not lose over five pounds. The size of the individual has something to do with how much he can lose.   One hundred twenty-three pound wrestlers cannot make as much weight as a one hundred seventy-seven pound wrestler.   Some men are able to take off more weight than others and still not suffer ill effects, but if it has a weakening effect they should give up the attempt.   Some wrestlers find that making a few pounds of weight increases their wrestling ability.   The wrestler himself should be the judge.

When a wrestler comes to the mat in first class shape for a match he has confidence in himself because he realizes what he can do at full strength.   On the other hand, one who comes to the mat after losing considerable weight cannot be sure how long his strength will last.

Weight Control

Post a weight chart in the dressing room which shows the weight of each man before and after workout.   This information can determine the individual weight reducing possibilities.   It also determines the weight class each man can wrestle in.

As the season approaches the wrestler's weight should be pretty well set and should be kept within a close range of the weight classification in which he intends to wrestle.   His diet must be balanced.   He must eat and drink enough fluids to keep his weight under control.

The following is an example of the weight making schedule for a college team.

WEIGHT CLASS	MONDAY	TUESDAY	WEDNES-DAY	THURSDAY	FRIDAY	MATCH SATURDAY
123 Lb. class	128	127	126	124½	123	123
130 Lb. class	135	134	133	131½	130	130
137 Lb. class	142	141	140	138½	137	137
147 Lb. class	152	151	150	148½	147	147
157 Lb. class	162	161	160	158½	157	157
167 Lb. class	172	171	170	168½	167	167
177 Lb. class	182	181	180	178½	177	177
Heavyweight class	EAT NORMALLY					HW *

The coach should set up a weight making schedule for the team and have them follow it very closely.   If a match is to be on Saturday, they should start on Monday, gradually reducing their weight until they are down to flat weight Friday evening.   They should consume about a pound and a half of food that evening.   The next morning before breakfast the weight should be checked. A quarter of a pound over does no harm as it can be lost by weighing-in time.

Chain Wrestling

Only the advanced student in wrestling can master enough maneuvers from a particular hold.   Every time a move is started he must know where it leads and what counter can be used against that maneuver.   He must be in position to counter that counter immediately.   If he is a smart wrestler he will have a counter to every counter; there is no end to the road.   A clever wrestler will try to lead his opponent into a trap.   Thus in chain wrestling there is no end to the number of moves that can progress from one particular hold.

Strategy

Every member of a wrestling squad must know and understand all the rules. A good many wrestlers have lost a close decision because of a simple infraction of the rules.

When preparing for a tough match wrestler A should have a thorough knowledge of his opponent's (wrestler B) tactics and characteristics.   A should spend considerable time in his work-outs on counters against B's favorite holds.   At the same time A must realize that B has made a thorough study of him and will have a counter for A's counter.   It is a matter of A working out his patterns against B so that he can stay one jump ahead of B.   This is difficult if his opponent is clever.   If A can find out how B sets them up, when he sets them up, and what he does in a pinch, then A's task to prepare for B is much simpler.

A must remember that his opponent knows the same things about him and that B is preparing to counter A's moves.   This leads him to a point where he must know what counters he is going to expect B to use against his own favorite maneuvers.   A must acquire a good counter for B's counter.   Wrestler A must always anticipate what his own maneuver can lead to and try to know the answers.

When meeting an opponent who is strong, but short in build, A can assume wrestler B has certain weaknesses.   Usually a man with these characteristics has short muscles; he seems to tire quickly and lose his complete sense of balance in the closing minutes of a hard match.   However, he is tough in the first minutes of a match.   Wrestler A should not take chances with B or he may be forced into a very bad position that will waste his energy.   In such a case B has then been able to force A to wrestle the pattern of the match as B wants it.   A should never wrestle his opponent's match, but should force B to waste his energy.   Then while B is tiring, A can shoot and beat him.

When A has studied his opponent's weaknesses thoroughly, he must plan his attack.   If B is not in condition, A can force B to waste his energy and then A can proceed to beat B in the last part of the match.   A wrestler must always keep in mind what has transpired during the match.   He must know what holds are working and those that are not.   Every move must count or he is wasting his energy.

After taking an opponent to the mat, wrestler A should proceed to tie B up while he is off balance.   If B has a chance to regain his balance, he will maneuver to get away.   If A needs to regain his wind after shooting hard it should be done while B is under A's control.   He must always plan to wrestle his matches by spurts as it is impossible to shoot all the way against a tough opponent.

A should keep his opponent tied up and force him to waste his energy.   He may become panicky and throw himself open to pin holds.   Wrestler A must take his time when applying pin holds, to be sure he won't lose his balance and get caught.   This is especially important when his opponent is fresh.   A should hold B there and gradually apply the pressure, forcing B to expend all his energy.   Gradually A will wear B down to where he can be pinned.   A must always keep his balance and make B carry his weight.

There will be a crucial moment in a match, perhaps during the later stages of a bout, when A may be behind in points.   At this crucial stage he must keep a cool head.   He may have to turn his opponent loose and give another point for escape.   This is good strategy if he is clever at take downs.   If he can score a take down he has regained one point.   Usually while scoring a take down, an opponent leaves himself open to pin holds.   This may give A an opportunity to score a near fall or get a pin and win the match.

A well versed wrestler must have respect for his opponent but yet have confidence in his own ability.   When a wrestler is over-confident he is apt to get careless and take undue chances.   If he is meeting a good opponent it may cost him the match.

Getting Ready for the Match

The way a wrestler prepares for a meet can make or break him; this is a very important stage of wrestling. If he overworks he comes to the mat tired for his match and as a result, his reflexes are slow.   Many matches have been lost in the last few days of practice.

If the match is to be wrestled on Saturday, the last hard workout should be on Wednesday evening.   Thursday, the workout should be cut in half, more stress laid on the opponent's weakness and how to take advantage of it.   Friday, the wrestler should come to the mat and work just enough to break a sweat and go in.   All during this period of preparation, he must follow the weight-reducing schedule closely.   After the workout Friday evening his weight must be down to flat weight and he is ready to eat a good meal.   The wrestler will be feeling at his lowest ebb at this time both physically and mentally.   He will now begin to re gain his strength and by match time he should reach peak performance.

Weighing-In

Saturday morning before breakfast the squad should report to the gym and check weight.   A wrestler can weigh from one fourth to one half pound over at this time.   If under weight, he must eat enough to make a fourth of a pound over; if over-weight, he should don sweat clothes and break a sweat until the weight is down.

The weight should be checked again about thirty minutes before weighing time.   If the weight is under, he can drink a little fruit juice and build the weight up to the proper weight class.   The scales must balance.   The wrestler should size up his opponent while he weighs in.

If the match is away from home, the same process should be followed.   However, if he travels all the way on the day of the match, the weight must be checked before he leaves.   A man can lose from a quarter to a half pound on a short trip.

Food, Water and Rest Before Match

Immediately upon weighing in, the wrestler who has made considerable weight should drink some fruit juice and take on a little water in order to replace the water lost by dehydration.   Weighing in five hours before a match permits him to eat a good meal.   This allows sufficient time for a carefully selected meal to digest.

Any foods that do not digest easily and quickly should be avoided, such as pastries and greasy foods.   There will be certain types of food that do not agree with an athlete and he should abstain from eating them.

This is a typical meal for a wrestler to eat before a match: small broiled steak or roast beef, baked potatoes, peas, one fourth head of lettuce with no dressing on it, apple sauce, fruit, two slices of toast, and cup of hot tea, well sugared.   This meal should be eaten very slowly.   Well-chewed food digests more easily.   (Refer to Chapter III.)

After the meal is completed the coach should take the team for a walk and then get them off their feet.   They may go to a movie or to bed.   Sometimes members of the team will lie in bed and worry about the match.   If a coach has a team of this type, it would be better to take them to a good movie.   The main thing is to get the match off their minds.

Just Before the Match

The team should report to the dressing room one hour before match time, weighing within three pounds of weight if they have eaten properly.   They must not drink excessive water before a match as it adds more weight to carry around.

The manager should have all the match equipment laid out for the team so they don't have to worry about getting it ready.   They should strip and put on sweat pants.   The room must be warm.   Each member of the team should have a rub down, starting with the light weight and going up the weight classes.   The entire team can massage on one wrestler at a time.   He should lie on his stomach and be rubbed on the back side for two minutes and then turn over and be rubbed on his front side for two minutes.   This gives each member of the team a four minute rub.   Then he can put on his sweat pants and help massage the rest of the team.   This process helps to get the entire team warmed up and lets them enjoy themselves at the same time.   It keeps them relaxed and has a tendency to keep their minds off the match.   When all rub-downs are completed, they can dress for the match and take a good warm-up.

The coach should talk to them about five minutes, building up confidence but reminding them to have respect for the opponent.   It is too late to give any technical knowledge.

They should now be ready to go on the mat.   If their training has been hard, and their efforts earnest, and the weight has been taken off gradually, they should be in first rate condition to wrestle a hard match with the greatest of confidence.

The Match

About ten minutes before his bout comes up the wrestler should start warming up (with his sweat clothes on) by doing his regular exercises.   During this process of warming up the wrestler should break a light sweat and keep it until the match begins.   This process is merely preparing the cardiorespiratory system so it can adjust itself to the load that it must carry during the match.

A should now be ready to come to the mat for his match, and if his training has been hard and he has acquired a thorough knowledge of the sport he will step from his corner with complete confidence in himself and in his ability to defeat his adversary.   If wrestler A has developed superior knowledge and skill he should be able to dominate the bout from the very start and force B to wrestle according to A's own plan.   A must make his opponent recognize that A is the master of the situation.   Once he has accomplished this the match is half won.

Every wrestler must realize that sometimes breaks will go against him during a match and that he will be behind in points.   He must think of this as being only a temporary situation and he must try to regain lost ground immediately.

Once defeat is accepted the cause is lost.   The wrestler must keep trying; never accept defeat even though it appears inevitable.   It is better to take a chance and try to win than to give up and lose without trying.   He must always remember if he comes to the mat in top condition and begins to tire, his adversary will tire too and one more explosive effort might win the match.

After the Match

The wrestler must always be a good sport and congratulate his opponent, win or lose.   He should rinse out his mouth and take a few swallows of water. Then put on his sweat clothes immediately to eliminate the possibility of catching cold.

As soon as the meet is over, he should take a hot shower and taper off with a cool one.   Bruises, scratches, and breaks in the skin should be cared for before leaving the dressing room because of the danger of infection.   The body must be thoroughly dried and cooled off before leaving.   He should eat a fair meal, take a walk, and go to bed.

The coach should evaluate every match, writing down each wrestler's mistakes and his good points.   At the next practice he will be able to discuss the good and bad points about each wrestler and outline the fundamentals that should be stressed during the coming week of practice.

the prevention and care of injuries

Athletics can be a great contributing factor to the health of the participants if carried on under the guidance of well-trained individuals. The regular habits during training season, proper foods, regular sleeping hours, and exercise following adequate training periods are all health aids. On the other hand athletics cannot be justified as an aid to health if its devotees are confronted by impaired health or disability when safety precautions are not followed. Many of the injuries that occur in an athletic program can be avoided if the coaches will, first, provide for a proper warming-up period, and second, make sure the conditioning program has been gradual. This will not only prevent pulled and overstrained muscles but will develop a more alert group of athletes.

No sport should be placed on a school's athletic program unless it can meet these qualifications: a well trained coach, adequate equipment, proper training facilities, a sufficient number of reserves, equitable competition, and good officiating for the sport. If the school can meet these qualifications it can carry on the sport both safely and sanitarily.

Sanitation and Safety Suggestions for Wrestling

Ordinarily the wrestlers are fine physical specimens with almost perfect physiques. By the time they have finished their school career they should have learned how to play; to give and take; to be good sportsmen; to co-operate; and above all, they should know how to live and take care of themselves physically. When the rules of safety and sanitation are violated, some of the most valuable "carry-over" lessons of athletics are lost.

The following is a list of suggestions for safety and sanitation. They may be used as a check list by the novice coach or manager:

1. Keep the mats smooth and cover tight.
2. See that mats and covers are kept clean and sanitary.
3. Be sure the walls are well padded around the mats or mats kept far enough away from walls.
4. Have a first aid kit on hand and someone trained to use it.
5. Give immediate attention to all injuries and infections.
6. Assure proper warm-up periods for all wrestlers.
7. Be sure all wrestlers are properly conditioned.
8. All wrestlers should have access to a wrestling helmet.
9. Have practice sessions well supervised and not too long.

10. Allow no one who is injured to participate unless he has a physician's permit.
11. They must have proper personal equipment.
12. Give proper attention to diet.
13. Study weight charts carefully.
14. Do not let anyone participate unless he has had a thorough physical examination.
15. Do not let any wrestler go to the extreme on weight making.
16. Keep all personal equipment sterilized.
17. Be sure all participants are cooled off and thoroughly dried before leaving locker room.
18. Insist on clean, dry towels every day.
19. Provide proper facilities for spitting.
20. Insist on a warm shower followed by a cool one for each participant.
21. Keep dressing room, lockers, and showers scientifically clean.
22. Provide sanitary drinking facilities.
23. Don't allow them to lie on mats and cool off quickly.
24. Provide a warm mat room for squads to work out in.

The Place of Coach and Trainer

The experience of the trainer and coach determines how far they may go in treating injuries. Neither of these individuals is qualified as a doctor and they must remember that first aid treatment should be exactly what the name implies. All diagnosis and medical treatment should be placed in the hands of a physician. In such cases as illness and disability the physician should decide when the patient may return to practice.

The Most Common Wrestling Injuries

These are a few injuries which occur most often in wrestling and others that are common in all sports. In the past few years a number of these injuries have been practically eliminated through rule changes that eliminate the dangerous holds; and through the great improvement in equipment and protective devices; and with better coaching. These injuries are discussed as follows: (1) mat burns, (2) cauliflower ears, (3) impetigo, (4) boils, (5) bruises, (6) sprains, (7) broken bones and dislocations, (8) pulled ribs, (9) athlete's foot.

Mat Burns

The use of the present-day plastic mat covers has reduced mat burns to a minimum. However, the skin of the novice is tender and he frequently burns his elbows, knees, or shoulders. Such an injury is the result of the outer layer of skin being rubbed off down to a bleeding or oozing surface.

Prevention: Mat burns can be prevented by keeping the elbows, knees and shoulders covered during workouts. After the skin becomes toughened it will not be necessary to wear covering.

Treatment: The wound should be thoroughly cleaned with warm water and a mild soap, followed with a light coat of 5 per cent sulfathiazole in a vanishing cream base, covered with a sterile gauze bandage. This should prevent any secondary infections or a large scab which will crack easily and retard healing. A neglected mat burn can cause serious infection which will require treatment by a physician.

Cauliflower Ears

This type of injury is caused by a hard blow, rubbing or rolling on the external ear. The skin separates from the cartilage of the ear and bleeding starts between this separation. This forms a pocket of blood and fluid, and if not treated it will harden. Such disfigurement will resemble a cauliflower.

Prevention: The best way to prevent this condition is to provide every member of the wrestling squad with a helmet and see that he wears it. Another way is to discourage the use of holds around the head, such as head locks and the rubbing of heads together. There are several kinds of helmets that are being used today. One well-designed helmet on the market today gives almost perfect protection. It has a plastic cup that fits snugly over the ears and is attached over the head and under the chin with elastic straps.

Treatment: To prevent the blood between the skin and cartilage from hardening, the blood from under the skin must be drawn out by use of a hypodermic needle. In order to restore the ear to normal thickness and contour, it may require several aspirations before the hemorrhage is finally checked. Because of the danger of infection if the needle is not properly sterilized, it should be done by a physician. Once the swelling has been relieved by the removal of the fluid, pressure must be applied to keep the skin and cartilage of the ear pressed tightly together. This is done with built-up layers of collodion and cotton filling the auricle of the ear. While preparing these applications, pressure must be kept on the ear or there will be a rapid influx of fluid which will have to be removed before applying the collodion treatment. This pressure must be kept on the ear for some time and every precaution must be taken against re-injury.

Impetigo

This is an inflammatory skin disease characterized by a small elevation of the cuticle filled with pus. It can be contracted by wrestling on unsanitary mats or with someone who has the infection.

Prevention: Do not permit anyone to wrestle who has an infectious skin disease and keep all equipment clean and sanitary. If these sanitary precautions are carried out, impetigo can be eliminated. However, once the wrestling area has been exposed, mat covers and every piece of wrestling gear must be taken up and washed in a strong antiseptic solution.

Treatment: Impetigo may be treated by several methods. However, the most common procedure used by athletic trainers is to clean the infected areas with 1/2000 mercuric chloride solution. After drying, apply a 10 per cent ammoniated mercury ointment.   This will cure an ordinary case of impetigo after a few days of treatment.   If these applications do not take care of the infection or if the patient has a very thin and tender skin, it should be treated by a physician.   Where impetigo is on the face, avoid shaving until the infection disappears.   This will reduce the chance of spreading the disease.

Boils

A boil is a localized staphylococcus infection of the skin.*   This infection may enter through a sweat gland or a hair follicle or it may start in a small cut, scratch or skin abrasion.

Prevention: The same as for impetigo.

Treatment: The first thing to do in treating a boil is to clean the boil and all the surrounding area by washing this area with mild soap or alcohol on sterile cotton.   Allow to dry and prepare a gauze pad large enough to cover the boil generously.   Then place on the pad a thick layer of athletic ointment and place over the boil and strap down with tape.   This treatment should be repeated each day until the boil is open, the core removed, and the wound is healed.   The surrounding area should be kept clean and coated with benzoin solution.   By all means do not let a boil get bruised.   If an athlete gets a series of boils consult a physician.

Bruises

Most of the bruises that happen in wrestling occur around the knee and elbow joints.   This usually happens when a wrestler drops down on his knees and elbows so suddenly that the mats are unable to absorb the force.

Prevention: The best way to prevent such injuries is to have the knees or elbows covered with a foam rubber pad.   Wrestlers should refrain from using maneuvers that cause the bruise until bruised areas have healed.

Treatment: Ice packs should be applied to the area immediately in order to limit hemorrhage and swelling.   Heat should be applied to the area the next day only.   After a few days the area around the bruise may be massaged lightly, but heat applications should be continued.

Sprains

Sprains are the most serious of the common injuries seen in athletics.   The treatment depends on the severity of the sprain.   In many cases tendons and ligaments are torn and without X-ray it is hard to differentiate between a sprain and a fracture.   All injuries of this type should be seen by a physician.

Prevention: The mat cover must always be taut, this will prevent feet getting tangled in the cover.   Weak ankles, wrists, elbows, knees and shoulders should be taped for protection.

---

*See Cramer, *Training Room Manual*, Gardner, Kansas, 1945, p. 113.

Treatment: As soon as the injury is recognized as a sprain, it should be wrapped with a compression bandage and placed in ice water or an ice pack should be applied. This will keep swelling down to a minimum and greatly reduce the period of convalescence. For the remainder of the day the patient should not use the injured part. If it is a severe sprain it should be immobilized for several days. However, the injured part should be used as soon as possible to prevent the formation of adhesions. Heat treatment should begin the day after the injury and continue until the sprain has healed. The sprain should be stripped with adhesive tape that is kept on for some time after the sprain has fully healed. This tape will protect the wrestler's injury from further damage when he is working out.

Broken Bones and Dislocations

If there is any question about a broken bone or dislocation, keep the injured person warm and comfortable. Call a physician and have him treat the injury. Never move him unless it is absolutely necessary.

Pulled Ribs

It is not uncommon for ribs to get pulled in wrestling, particularly with the use of certain holds around the ribs. A pulled rib is merely the separation of the rib from the cartilage.

Prevention: Avoid trying to twist the body in holds that are extremely tight around the rib section.

Treatment: The best method is to tape the ribs with two-inch adhesive tape to give relief and permit healing. Have the injured man stand and do the taping while he is exhaling, Start the taping at the back bone and continue on around until it is about four inches beyond center in front. The first piece of tape should start about four inches above the injury. Continue with the taping until reaching an area about four inches below the injury. It will take about six weeks for recovery. When he returns for practice the ribs should be kept taped until he feels safe without it.

Athlete's Foot

It is a fungus infection in the skin usually found between the toes. The symptoms are itching, redness between the toes, or the presence of small blisters over the heel and sole of the foot. It is a very common infection and can lead to disability if not treated.

Prevention: The feet should be dried thoroughly after each shower. The dressing room and shower should be clean and well ventilated, using a strong solution of lysol.

Treatment: If there are signs of athlete's foot use Sopronal or Desenex powder on the affected area. Put this powder on in the morning and follow at night with Sopronal or Desenex ointment. This will take care of an ordinary case of athlete's foot. However, if there are signs of secondary infection it is best to see a physician.

the administration of competition

The coach needs to give considerable attention to the administration of meets. Intelligent planning is essential if the meets are to be businesslike, attractive, and well-organized sports events. In many cases the reputation of the coach may be measured by the manner in which the contest is conducted. A meet that is well managed is recognized for its educational value and good sportsmanship. The coach must not only work for the welfare of his own wrestlers but he must be responsible for the welfare of the opposition. He must recognize the importance of sound publicity and make wise use of showmanship devices. The officials for a wrestling contest must be very carefully selected, as they play an important part in how smoothly a meet is conducted.

The School's General Athletic Policies and Functions

If any athletic department is to function well, it must operate on sound, well-established administration policies. Do not formulate policies as problems arise. All staff members, athletes, and the director should be familiar with general policies of the department. The policies are not allied with any one particular sport but concern the whole program. Usually such policies must have the approval of the Athletic Board.

Student Managers: For a student manager system to operate satisfactorily the athletic department should set up a few guiding rules. These rules should include the method of selection, the system of rewards and recognition, and a general outline of the manager's duties. A student manager will be more than glad to be of service to the team and will appreciate the opportunity to learn by doing.

Banquets: A definite policy should be set up in regard to banquets; either have it every year or not at all. The banquet should not depend upon the success of the squad. It is just as important to fete a losing team as a winning team. If they have had a poor season their morale is down and they will need the added lift. The banquet should be a school or community affair. However, the athlete must be made to realize early in his career that the school owes him nothing.

Awards: There should be a definite policy and participation requirement set up for wrestling as well as for other sports. The awards should be the same for all sports. After all, we are trying to teach democratic ideals and principles in all sports. The candidate for awards should know the school policy and the requirements for an award. A participation record should be kept on each individual.   At the end of the season the coach should make his recommendation to the athletic director, and then get the approval of the athletic board.

Equipment: The purchase and care of wrestling equipment represents one of the major problems confronting a coach.   The purchase of wrestling equipment should not be done haphazardly.   A certain time should be set aside for this important transaction.   At the close of each season an inventory should be taken.   From this inventory the coach can tell what equipment has to be replaced or repaired, and what new equipment is needed.

The equipment that needs repair should be taken care of immediately.   When new equipment is needed the coach should give the athletic director a list of the equipment, with specifications, so it can be ordered as soon as the money is available.   This will give the sporting goods company ample time for delivery.

Finance and Budget: The financial management of his sport is a very important duty of a coach.   He is always handling money and making financial transactions.   At the end of each wrestling season he should present a proposed budget for the coming season.   He takes into consideration the cost of new equipment, lodging on trips, meals, cost of officials, contracts for home contests, transportation, medical expense, tickets, laundry, etc.   He must also consider gate receipts, contracts for away-from-home games, and any other income.   Past records can give him a good idea of what to expect.

Schedules: These should be made out at least a year in advance.   The home contests should be alternated with those away from home as near as possible.   Be sure they do not interfere with class periods or other school functions.   The number of wrestling meets for a high school should be from six to eight while a college can have from eight to ten meets each year.   Contracts should be made out in duplicate, signed by both schools, with each school keeping a copy.   It should specify the date, the basis of contract, and the forfeit clause.

Contracting Officials: Great care should be taken in selecting officials.   The success of the meet depends upon them to a large extent.   The officials should be secured from six months to a year in advance of the contest.   The home school should submit a list of officials to the visiting school for approval.   When the approval has been given the official should be secured and his contract signed.

Permanent Records of Eligibility, Participation, and Results: Just as soon as school begins in the fall the coach should check the eligibility of his wrestling squad.   The state athletic association or the institution should provide forms for this purpose.   If they do not, then some should be devised.   Each member of the squad should be passed upon by the school authorities.

During the season, a record of each meet should be kept and filed.   At the end of the season the complete results of the meets should be made up.   From this form the participation record can be completed and the recommendation for awards made.

General Reports: These reports should be made for the permanent records and should be brief but complete.   These general reports should include at least the (1) results of meets (2) number of participants (3) the outstanding accomplishments of the wrestling season (4) a financial statement (5) proposed schedule for the next year.

Responsibilities in Preparing for a Wrestling Season:

1. Arrange for dual meet schedule.
2. Draw up contracts with other schools.
3. Make contracts with officials for home meets.
4. Get the approval of schedule by director and athletic board.
5. Set date for the beginning of practice, and time of daily practice.
6. Work out practice schedule.
7. Check on general equipment such as mats, mat covers, scales, and sweat room.
8. Order personal equipment.
9. Secure training room supplies.
10. Secure trainer and team physician.
11. Announce when equipment will be checked out.
12. Check on eligibility of squad members.
13. Have squad members report for physical examination.
14. Get out publicity on squad.
15. Check on score board.
16. Get public address system in shape.
17. Secure someone to handle public address system.
18. Secure scorer and timers.
19. Have photograph made of team.
20. Check on home schedule and be sure it does not conflict with other sports.
21. Arrange for hotel reservations for all meets.
22. Secure transportation for meets away from home.
23. Secure the following pieces of equipment:
    A. Stop watches
    B. Whistles
    C. Horn
    D. Rule books
    E. Weight charts
    F. Scales
    G. Dual meet score sheets
    H. Jumping ropes
    I. Drinking water facilities
    J. Buckets to be used as cuspidors.

Responsibilities the Week Before Meet:

1. Notify visiting team coach of the hour, date of meet, and weighing in time.
2. Have visiting team send roster of team, photos for programs, and publicity purposes.

3. Notify officials as to date and time of meet.
4. Print programs.
5. Get eligibility list of own team members.
6. Notify manager to have all equipment ready and give him a list of team for suiting-up purposes.
7. Have manager get all meet equipment ready.
8. Conduct tryouts for team.
9. Get towels and dressing room ready for visiting team.
10. Have officials' dressing room ready.
11. If meet is away from home make the following arrangements:

    A. Procure money for trips
    B. Check on hotel reservations
    C. Have transportation ready
    D. Make arrangements for special menus
    E. Notify opposing coach when you expect to arrive
    F. Make arrangements for workout and the use of scales
    G. Post travel list, time of departure and where leaving from
    H. Notify administration how long the team will be gone
    I. Have team members arrange with instructors for class work to be made up
    J. Get each team member to check to see if personal equipment is packed
    K. Manager must see that all equipment is packed and loaded.

Responsibilities on the Day of Meet:

1. Order special menus to be eaten after weighing-in.
2. Have scales ready for weighing-in.
3. Have dual meet scoring sheets ready to use at weighing-in time. (Fig. 4)
4. Check with scorer, and timer to see if they will be available.
5. Arrange timer and scorer table.
6. Get mats and cover set up for meet.
7. Have bucket, towels, and water available at mat corners for each team.
8. Have dressing rooms ready for visiting team and officials.
9. Arrange for distribution of programs for meet. (Fig. 5)
10. Set up and test public address system.
11. Be sure scoreboard is ready and have someone to operate it.
12. Test lighting and ventilation of gymnasium.
13. Be sure bleachers are checked for safety.
14. Instruct manager to have towels ready for visiting team and coach.
15. All personal equipment must be ready for team.
16. Be sure trainer, physician, and rubbing tables are ready.
17. Have someone responsible for equipment such as watches, whistles, horn, rule book, score sheets, etc.
18. Be sure the press and photographer are taken care of.

WRESTLING MEET

_____ VS. _____   _____ DATE _____   _____ TIME _____   _____ REFEREE _____

WEIGHT CLASS	WRESTLERS	TEAM	DEC.	FALL	SCORE₁		REMARKS
			POINTS	TIME			
123							
130							
137							
147							
157							
167							
177							
H. W.				TOTAL			

OFFICIAL SCORER _____

Figure 4

WRESTLING MEET

AUBURN VS MEMPHIS NAVY

FEBRUARY 23, 1952

WEIGHT CLASS	WRESTLERS	HOME TOWN	TEAMS	POINT SCORE		TEAM SCORE	
				DEC.	FALL	AUBURN	MN
123 lbs.	Robert David VS Jerry McAdoo	Birmingham, Ala. Pittsburg, Pa.	Auburn Memphis Navy				
130 lbs.	Ray Downey VS Dick Miller	Birmingham, Ala. Wahoo, Neb.	Auburn Memphis Navy				
137 lbs.	James Johns VS Fred LaBlanc	Frisco City, Ala. Syracuse, N. Y.	Auburn Memphis Navy				
147 lbs.	Jerry Bains VS Paul Olson	Oneonta, Ala. Clarion, Iowa	Auburn Memphis Navy				
157 lbs.	Russell Baker VS Bob Montgomery	Vicksburg, Miss. Council Bluffs, Iowa	Auburn Memphis Navy				
167 lbs.	Fred Shaw VS John Perrine	Chattanooga, Tenn. Oil City, Pa.	Auburn Memphis Navy				
177 lbs.	John Glenn VS Cole Black	Pelham, Ga. Lake City, Minn.	Auburn Memphis Navy				
Hvy. Wt.	Dan McNair VS Merle Wilson	New Orleans, La. Clarion, Iowa	Auburn Memphis Navy				
					TOTAL		

COACHES:

Swede Umbach—Auburn
Wesley Brown, Jr.—Memphis Navy

REFEREE: Julius Palone—Arkansas State College

TEAM SCORE:	BOUT SCORING:	
Fall—5 points	Takedown—2 points	Time Advantage—
Decision—3 points	Reverse—2 points	1 point per minute
Draw—2 points	Near Fall—2 points	Maximum—2 points
	Escape—1 point	

AUBURN'S REMAINING SCHEDULE

Feb. 28 & 29—Southeastern Intercollegiate Wrestling Championships—Emory University

Figure 5

Responsibilities After the Meet:

1. Payment of officials.
2. Pay visiting school the contract guarantee.
3. Make out report on official twenty-four hours after the meet.
4. Finish out the score sheet and file it.
5. Have manager collect all equipment used for the meet and store it away.
6. Give the team a fair meal and send them to bed.
7. Thank all those who had a part in running off the meet.
8, Be sure all courtesies are extended to visitors.

The Organization and Planning of a Wrestling Tournament:

The date for the wrestling tournament is usually set by the coaches a year in advance.   About six weeks before the tournament a letter should go out to all competing schools as a reminder of the date, time, and location of the tournament (Fig. 6).

The local committee to aid the tournament manager in administering the meet should be composed of eleven men with duties as follows:

Tournament manager and assistant manager:

1. Wrestling officials should be contracted within thirty days of the meet. At least one referee will be needed for each mat.
2. Entry blanks containing all necessary information should be prepared and mailed about thirty days preceding the meet (Fig. 7).
3. One team of three timers should be assigned to each mat.   One team to each referee.
4. There should be one scorer for each mat.
5. Arrange for physician to be on duty at all sessions and to check for communicable diseases at the weighing-in.
6. Be sure that all medals are ready to be presented at the finals.   This should also include the team trophy.
7. Rubber stamps should be present at weighing-in time so that all contestants may be stamped for identification purposes.
8. Bout cards should be printed for recording results for each bout.   These cards are signed by the referee and official scorer at the conclusion of each match (Fig. 8).
9. An official team scoring chart should be prepared for recording the official team scores (Fig. 9).
10. Brackets for the drawing should be mimeographed for the use of the rules committee in making the drawing.
11. Be sure to have numbers and shaker available for the drawing.
12. Send out entry forms for all weight classes, receive entries, and collect entry fees.

(Continued on page 231).

Southeastern Intercollegiate Wrestling Championships March 7 & 8, 1952

PLACE—Sports Arena, Alabama Polytechnic Institute, Auburn, Alabama.

DATE AND TIME—Friday, March 7th.   2:00 p. m. and 7:30 p. m.
                Saturday, March 8th.   2:00 p. m. and 7:30 p. m.

ADMISSION PRICES—(Tax Included)

Preliminaries	Friday, 2:00 p. m.	$.75
Quarter Finals	Friday, 7:30 p. m.	.75
Semi-Finals	Saturday, 2:00 p. m.	.75
Finals	Saturday, 7:30 p. m.	1.00
Reserved Seat Season Ticket		2.50

RULES—

The tournament will be governed by the National Intercollegiate Rules.

WEIGHTS—

Weights contested will be 115, 123, 130, 137, 147, 157, 167, 177, 191, and Heavyweight.

UNIFORMS—

The uniform shall consist of full-length tights, with outside close fitting short trunks and shirt.

ELIGIBILITY—

The contestants must be eligible under the rules specified by the National Collegiate Athletics Association.

WEIGHING-IN—

Time—9:00 a. m., both days at the Sports Arena.   One pound overweight shall be allowed the second day.

MATS—

Two mats will be available for all sessions.

AWARDS—

Standard Intercollegiate medals will be awarded to first, second, and third place winners in each weight class.   A handsome trophy will be presented to the team winning the championships.   A trophy will be awarded to the outstanding wrestlers.

ENTRIES—

Entries close Monday, March 3, 1952 at 6:00 p.m. with Al Martincic, tournament manager, Alumni Gymnasium, Auburn, Alabama.

ENTRY FEES—

None

EXPENSES—

Absolutely no expenses will be paid contestants or teams.

TOURNAMENT PHYSICIAN—

The Director of the Student Health Service of Alabama Polytechnic Institute will be the physician for the meets.

ENTRY BLANKS—

The enclosed entry blanks must be in our hands by Monday, March 3, 1952.

HOUSING ACCOMMODATIONS—

The Housing Department of Alabama Polytechnic Institute can provide sleeping accommodations at a charge of $1.00 per person per night.   There are two good hotels within walking distance of the Sports Arena.

MEALS—

Available at Magnolia Hall cafeteria at reasonable rates.

TOURNAMENT MANAGEMENT—

Management of this tournament will be in the hands of the Athletic Department of Alabama Polytechnic Institute, duly appointed representative of the Southeastern Intercollegiate Wrestling Association.

Figure 6

Official Entry Blank

Southeastern Intercollegiate Wrestling Association
Sports Arena

Alabama Polytechnic Institute, Auburn, Alabama
March 7 & 8, 1952

Entries close March 3, 1952. (Please type, include full name—last, first, and middle initial.

115 lbs. _____   _____
                    Name   Name

123 lbs. _____   _____
                    Name   Name

130 lbs. _____   _____
                    Name   Name

137 lbs. _____   _____
                    Name   Name

147 lbs. _____   _____
                    Name   Name

157 lbs. _____   _____
                    Name   Name

167 lbs. _____   _____
                    Name   Name

177 lbs. _____   _____
                    Name   Name

191 lbs. _____   _____
                    Name   Name

Heavyweight _____   _____
                    Name   Name

CERTIFICATION

We certify that the listed contestants are eligible under the rules specified by the National Collegiate Athletic Association to represent

_____   _____
Name of Institution   Address of Institution

_____   _____
Registrar   Chairman, Faculty Committee

_____
Wrestling Coach

Figure 7

Southeastern Intercollegiate Wrestling Championships
March 3 & 4, 1950
Auburn, Alabama

BOUT NO _____ MAT NO _____ ROUND _____

TEAMS	WRESTLERS	DECISIONS	FALL	WINNER

WEIGHT CLASS_____ REFEREE_____

Figure 8

Southeastern Intercollegiate Wrestling Championships
Emory University, Atlanta, Georgia
February 28 & 29, 1952

TEAMS	FALLS	FIRST PLACE	SECOND PLACE	THIRD PLACE	FOURTH PLACE	TOTAL SCORE
1.						
2.						
3.						
4.						
5.						
6.						
7.						
8.						
9.						
10.						
11.						
12.						

KEY TO SCORING FOR TOURNAMENTS

First place—6   Fourth place—1
Second place—4   For each fall
Third place—2   scored—1

Figure 9

(Continued from page 227).

13. Send out letter to all schools announcing conduct of meet arrangement as follows:
    A. Hotel accommodations and rates
    B. If college, what dormitory housing is available and rates
    C. Eating accommodations
    D. How towels and lockers will be handled
    E. Give dead-line for entries
    F. Get publicity material (photos, records, mats of individuals)
    G. Request that they advise tournament manager when they expect to arrive.
14. Have several student managers available to help.
15. Have money ready to pay officials after meet.

Manager of Equipment and Gear:
1. Locate the required number of 24' X 24' mats and covers that are needed for the meet (Fig. 10).
2. Have four stop watches for each mat. Only three will be needed for each mat but one should be held in reserve.
3. Be sure that adequate locker facilities are available for all wrestlers. Keep team together, if possible.
4. Two scales should be used during the weighing-in.
5. See that the proper number of administrative tables are placed in the proper place.
6. Have mats in place.

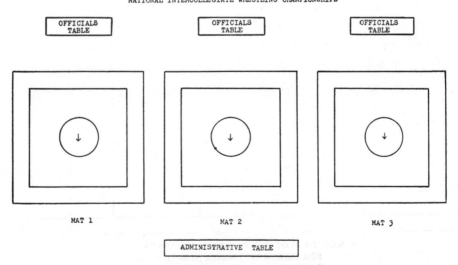

FLOOR PLAN FOR

NATIONAL INTERCOLLEGIATE WRESTLING CHAMPIONSHIPS

Fig. 10.—Floor Plan for National Intercollegiate Wrestling Championships.

7. Erect adequate score board for individual matches.
8. Have coaches' room ready for meeting.
9. Have dressing rooms for officials.

The Food and Housing Committee:

1. Make arrangements for sleeping quarters and eating accommodations before sending out entry blanks. This information should be included on the entry blanks.

The Reception Committee:

1. Serves as official host for all visiting schools.
2. Looks after the comfort and needs of visiting teams.
3. A number of student managers should be assigned to this task.
4. Arrange for a lounging room for officials and coaches.

Training and First Aid:

1. Trainer should be on duty throughout the meet.
2. Be sure training facilities are ready.

Meet Physicians:

1. To be at weighing-in to check contestants.
2. To be at all sessions of tournament.

The Announcer:

1. Responsible for setting up the public address system.
2. Should have a clear understanding as to what is to be handled over the public address system.
3. Must have a good background in wrestling.

The Business Manager:

1. Has full responsibility for the financial end of the tournament.
2, Have tickets and ticket taker ready.
3. Have a pass system set up so all contestants, coaches, and officials may get in.

The Meet Secretary:

1. Be sure to have brackets posted between each session of tournament.
2. Scoring by teams should be posted between sessions of the tournament.
3. Work out the order of bouts.
4. Have contestants notified before hand when their bout comes and on which mat.
5. Records results of each bout.
6. Keep teams' score, etc.
7. Should have several student managers to help out.
8. After the tournament make out a complete summary of the meet.

Publicity Director:

1. Request for pictures and publicity material should be sent to schools likely to enter outstanding wrestler.
2. Posters advertising the meet should be posted several weeks in advance.
3. Notify press and radio of tournament.
4. Make complete reports on progress of tournament.

Tournament Procedure:

Be sure all men on the local committee have thoroughly instructed the individuals assigned to them. If all members of the local committee do their respective jobs well, the tournament will go along smoothly. The tournament manager should be seated at the administrative table at.all sessions. He will then be in a position to anticipate problems and "troubleshoot" in any phase of the tournament.

Final Reports:

1. Financial report should be sent to national organization showing all guarantees, gross income of meet, receipts of expenditures, etc.
2. Report of the meet should be sent to the national organization with copies of forms and blanks used.
3. Make a report to the national rules committee for the wrestling guide.
4. Report to the next tournament manager with suggestions for improving tournament procedures.
5. Send out copies of completed tournament brackets to all coaches and officials who attended the meet.

facilities, equipment and safety devices

Today the maintenance and selection of equipment constitutes one of the major responsibilities of the wrestling coach. He should give considerable study and thought to the location of the mat room, the type of equipment needed, maintenance, and sanitation. With greater emphasis placed on safety, most coaches feel obligated to protect their players with adequate equipment. A well-dressed, well-equipped team appeals more to the public and at the same time suffers fewer injuries. The wrestling equipment that is needed to carry on a good program is inexpensive and will last many years.

The Mat Room

The wrestling room should be large, well-ventilated, and exposed to the direct sunlight for a good part of the day. There should be plenty of space for instruction. The mats should not crowd the walls unless they are well padded. If there are any columns in the room, these supports should be padded with mats to eliminate hazards. The floors should be of wood to give the participants better protection. Each individual participant should have approximately fifty square feet of space. Thus, an area of fifty feet by fifty feet could easily take care of a class of fifty participants. The greatest cause of injuries in wrestling is due to men falling over each other; for that reason alone it is desirable to have adequate space.

The Mats

Men have wrestled on the grass or soft spaded ground for hundreds of years. However, this hasn't proved very satisfactory, because there is too much chance for injuries. The best mats are made from number one hair felt mat filler, resilient, non-packing, and tufted about every nine inches. Wrestling mats should be at least two inches thick, preferably three inches, and should be covered with fifteen ounce to twenty-one ounce white duck material. Where mats are to be used for wrestling only, and are seldom moved, they should be at least twenty-four feet by twenty-four feet. However, if the mats are to be used for a large number of purposes, as they are in most gymnasiums, it is better to have them in four strips, each six feet by twenty-four feet. It is not wise to wrestle on the bare canvas mats, because the surface is coarse and will cause mat burns. Also, it is impossible to keep these mats clean and sanitary.

The Mat Cover

The type of cover used is very important.   It should be stretched tight on the mat to avoid wrinkles; this will cut down the number of injuries, since it is very easy for a wrestler to get his feet tangled in the cover.   The cover must also be kept clean to limit infection to a minimum.

The mat cover should extend at least one and one-half feet beyond the mat on all four sides.   If the mat is twenty-four feet by twenty-four feet, the cover should be at least twenty-seven feet by twenty-seven feet.   There should be grommets inserted in the outer edge of the mat cover.   The cover can be tightened by means of a cord interlaced between the grommets.

Listed below are the characteristics of the three most common types of covers used.

Canton flannel does not burn; easy to launder if the cover isn't too large; is not as durable as other types of covers.   It should be sprayed each day with a mild antiseptic solution.   This type of cover should be swept once a day, and it must be kept strictly sanitary.

Rubber does not burn; can easily be kept clean by washing it with a mild antiseptic solution; is durable.   The initial cost is quite high, but it will last for many years and probably is cheaper in the long run.   Many coaches object to this type of cover because it restricts the freedom of movement when sliding the feet on the cover.

Plastic probably the best and most popular cover used today.   It will not burn and will outlast any other cover on the market.   The traction is considered ideal.   The initial cost is high, but it is cheaper in the long run.   This cover must be kept tight or it may crack; however, it is easily repaired.   It can be washed by a mild antiseptic solution which makes it easy to keep sanitary.

Scales

A good set of platform scales is a very important piece of equipment for a wrestling squad.   They should register up to three hundred pounds and be easily read from either side.   The wrestler is more concerned about his weight than any other athlete.   He has to keep within a certain weight classification, and he should check his weight every day.

Cuspidors

The planners of a wrestling room should provide a cuspidor where it is easily available.   It should flush easily with a little water and be set in a recess in the wall.   This is essential since some wrestlers must expectorate during practice, and if no proper container is provided the wall or floor becomes the place.   At all tournaments and meets a bucket and towel should be made available for this purpose.

Personal Equipment

The wrestling squad should have two sets of equipment, one for practice and one for meet competition. It is important that every wrestler keep his equipment clean. Since wrestling is a contact sport, there is too much chance of passing infections from one individual to another. The equipment should be laundered often.

Practice equipment should consist of a pair of knitted wrestling trunks, soft rubber-soled shoes, sweat socks, and supporter. In the past few years the wrestling helmet has become a very important piece of equipment for practice. Each participant should be outfitted with a sweat suit to prevent his cooling off too rapidly.

Meet equipment: The uniform of each contestant should consist of full length tights with outside over-shorts fitted snugly and shirt with supporter attached. The shoes should be made of good grade lightweight canvas, with eyelet lace, high cut, with heelless rubber soles.

All members of the team should be dressed in the school colors, and each member provided with a woolen sweat suit.

principles of officiating

A wrestling official should come to the meet with a thorough knowledge of wrestling and its rules. A part of his philosophy should be to let a wrestling match progress with as little interference as possible on his part. The sport is confined to a close area; the actions are fast with constantly changing positions. Under these conditions the official must make split second decisions; they must be clear and concise.

In dual meets the point system can decide a match, while in a tournament this same system may fail him because there can be no draws; he must make a decision. Under these conditions he must keep an account of what has happened during the course of a match, because he might be called upon to make that all-important decision.

There was a time in this country when every section interpreted the rules differently, however, today there is more uniformity in rules. This is due primarily to the Official Wrestling Guide and the coaches' and officials' clinics held all over this country.

The material pertaining to officiating which appears in this chapter has been prepared in such a form that the official can easily take it from the pages and transfer it to his own code of standards in running off a wrestling meet.

Qualifications of Officials:

If one would study some of the best wrestling officials in this country he would find certain definite qualities that made them outstanding as officials. A young official can gain much valuable information by studying the techniques of these men, but these techniques should be adapted only so far as they fit his personality. These qualities will be discussed in the order of their importance.

Reaction Time: An official who works a wrestling meet must be on his toes at all times, and in the right place at the right time, to react at such situations or he may become lost in a mass of maneuvers. In a few seconds time, he may have to award six or seven points. A man who does not react quickly is not apt to become a very successful official.

Calmness: The official for a wrestling meet must be calm and cool, and never get excited. He is under great pressure. He must make decisions which are hairline and many could be called either way. He cannot pay attention to what spectators say. High-strung individuals should never referee wrestling matches as they can upset the equilibrium of the contestants and destroy the confidence that the public has in athletics in general. An official who is calm breeds confidence among the spectators and contestants; even though they disagree with his judgment, they will react more favorably and are more willing to co-operate.

Confidence: In order to develop confidence as an official, he must have a good background in wrestling, not only as a contestant, but also as a coach. By having lived close to the sport he can anticipate the moves of wrestlers and therefore be in a better position to make decisions. There should be no hesitation in his decisions, but they should be deliberate, rather than hasty. Decisions will be accepted by everyone if he makes them positive. Decisions should be given in a clear, strong voice, for a properly pitched tone carries conviction and breeds confidence.

Consistency: The official must set up certain definite rules and standards that will govern him in the exchange of positions and along the edge of the mat. This will make for consistency in decisions and breed confidence in his ability as an official. The official's decisions must be consistent when the same conditions or similar circumstances exist. Once the contestants see that the official has called them the same for both, they will continue the match with confidence.

Judgment: This can come only after years of experience as a contestant, as coach, and as an official. If the basic principles of wrestling are thoroughly understood, then sound judgment can be developed through experience in handling the contest. The official must set up sound principles along the edge of the mat, and during the exchange of position if he hopes to progress in judgment. Most of the errors that are made during the course of a wrestling match are at the edge of the mat and in the exchange of positions. Good judgment can be developed only through practice and experience.

Thorough Knowledge of Rules: There is no excuse for a wrestling official not knowing the rules. Anyone with average intelligence can learn the rules, the duties, and the mechanics of officiating. He can learn the rules by studying the Official Rules Guide and if there is any question on the interpretation of these rules, he can be straightened out at the Official Rules meeting. Simply knowing the rules does not guarantee good officiating, but it will help him in his interpretation of these rules. He must have the qualities already mentioned in this chapter if he hopes to be a successful official.

Condition: Any official must be in condition if he expects to be alert and to be able to give his best performance throughout a meet or a tournament. He should keep himself in good condition throughout the year and above all, he should be in top condition during the season. He should pay particular attention to endurance (heart and lungs) to ensure his readiness to meet any emergency.

Appearance: No official should try to play the part of a referee at wrestling meets unless he is willing to dress the part. He should secure the proper uniform and be sure that it fits. It should be neat and clean in appearance. The standard uniform for wrestling is white shirt and pants with black belt and shoes.

Referee's Pre-Meet Duties: The referee should arrive at the scene of the wrestling meet at least thirty minutes before meet time, dressed and ready to go. He should get the coaches together immediately and clarify the rules for them.

He should visit the dressing quarters of each team to check contestants and give the following instructions:

1.   Contestants must be inspected for improper clothing such as shirts with buttons at shoulder.   Be sure shirts are fastened at crotch.
2.   No objectional pads may be worn.
3.   Shoes must have eyelets and not hooks.
4.   All rings must be removed from fingers.
5.   Finger nails must be smooth and clipped short.
6.   Wrestlers must report to the center of the mat ready to wrestle (Fig. 11).
7.   Contestants are to shake hands and return to the edge of the circle until the referee's signal to start wrestling (Fig. 12).

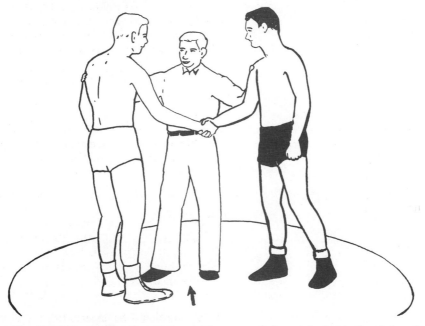

Fig. 11.—Referee calling the wrestlers to the center of the mat for instructions before the match starts.

He should perform the following duties at the Administrative table:

1.   See that the timers and scorers are properly seated.
2.   Instruct the head timer that he is in charge of the timers and scorers.
   A.   He is responsible for keeping the over-all time of the matches.
   B.   In case of an injury he is responsible for recording accumulated time out.

C. He should be able to notify the referee who has the position of advantage at the start of the third period.

D. He must notify the referee of any disagreement by the official scorer and time keepers only after an imminent situation has passed.

·E. He should assist the referee in determining whether a situation occurred before or after the termination of a period.

F. Each minute should be called to the referee, contestants, and spectators.

G. The last minute should be called out after fifteen-second intervals.

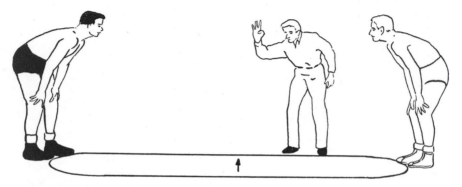

Fig. 12.—The position of the referee and wrestlers for starting a bout from standing position. Note the wrestlers are at the edge of the circle and referee is facing the official table.

The referee should give the following instructions to the assistant time-keepers:

1. Watches must be kept on table in view of all timers.

2. Record accumulative time advantage of the contestant to whom they are assigned when the referee indicates it.

3. Always check each others' time advantage recording.

4. Keep checking the head time keeper's recording.

5. Advise the head timer when any disagreement occurs regarding time advantage.

6. Show the referee the stop watches' recording of the time advantage each contestant has accumulated at the end of the match.

The referee should give the following instructions to the scorers:

1. Record the point score of both contestants during the course of the match when signaled by the referee.

2. Constantly check on each others' score reading.

3. Advise the head timer when they are in disagreement regarding the score.

4. Advise the scoreboard continuously of the official score during the match.

5. Must show the referee the score card at the end of each match.

The referee shall notify the timers and scorers as follows:

1. When the match begins.
2. When the match is stopped for any reason.
3. When the match is resumed.
4. The beginning of time advantage for contestant.
5. When time advantage stops for an individual.
6. When time out is called for any situation.
7. He shall notify the scorer when points are awarded and to whom.

Just before the meet is to begin the referee shall call the two captains to the center of the mat and toss a coin for choice of advantage position in split matches. In tournament matches the toss of the coin is made at the end of the first period if no fall occurs before that time.

When the match is to start the referee calls the contestants to the center of the mat where they shake hands and are given brief instructions: (1) they are not to stop wrestling until the referee blows his whistle; (2) they are to do most of their wrestling near the center circle of the mat. They then step back to a neutral position within the circle and wait for the signal to wrestle.

REFEREE TECHNIQUES DURING THE MATCH

While the Wrestlers Are on Their Feet: The referee blows a whistle to start the match. He must be facing the administrative table with the contestants, scorers, and timers in full view.

While the contestants are wrestling on their feet he should keep on a move from one side of the wrestlers to the other so he can get a view of both sides of the contestants. He should keep at a safe distance so he will not interfere with the progress of the bout, but should be close enough to control any unusual situations. It is particularly important that he assume the proper position along the edge of the mat as it is here that many important decisions are made. He must keep a constant lookout for any illegal position about the head and neck.

The referee should watch the following points closely while the wrestlers are on their feet:

1. Does the wrestler try to assume questionable positions on his opponent.
2. Does he play the edge of the mat.
3. Does he intentionally back off the mat.
4. Does he intentionally go off the mat to prevent a take down.
5. Is he pushed off or does he intentionally leave the mat.
6. Is he stalling on his feet by making no aggressive move.

The referee can make the meet a success by following the spirit and letter of the rules. He must enforce the rules rigidly if he expects to succeed as an official for wrestling meets.

Officiating While the Contestants Are on the Mat: The referee must be alert while the contestants are down on the mat as the positions change so fast. The wrestlers can become so entangled that it is hard to tell who has the advantage, particularly along the edge of the mat.   He must keep on a constant move from one side of the wrestlers to the other.

The referee shall start the match in referee position as follows (Fig. 13):

1. At the beginning of the second period.
2. At the beginning of the third period.
3. After the contestants go off the mat when one has the advantage (Fig. 14).
4. If the match is stopped because of injury when one has the advantage.
5. If the referee has to stop the match because of an illegal hold and the rules state there shall be a change of position.

Fig. 13.—The referee position for the underneath and top man to start wrestling on the mat. The referee is facing the wrestlers and the official tables.   The match is started by the sound of the whistle.

In starting the match from a referee's position the official shall assume a position in front of the wrestlers at a safe distance away so he will not interfere with the progress of the match.   He must face the officials' table while the wrestlers face him.

Before he starts the match he should observe the following points for the underneath man:

1. Are his hands, knees, and feet parallel to each other.
2. Are his hands at least one foot in front of his knees.
3. Are his hands flat on the mat.
4. Is he sitting still.

For the top man position:

1. Is his arm loose around the waist of his opponent.
2. Is his hand in the right position on his opponent's elbow.
3. Does his leg touch his opponent's leg.
4. Is his knee beyond his opponent's foot.
5. Is his head in a legal position.

Once the referee is sure the contestants have assumed the proper positions as indicated above he is ready to start the match by raising his hand to indicate to the timers and contestants that he is ready. He will then blow the whistle.

The referee should keep near the contestants at all times so that he may be ready for the following:

1. To block illegal holds (Fig. 14).
2. To determine whether the hold is punishing.
3. To determine when the wrestlers go off the mat (Fig. 15).
4. To see that reverses do not occur until one contestant has complete control over the other (Fig. 16).

Fig. 14.—The referee is in position to stop a hold from turning into an illegal hold which could injure one of the participants.

5. To see that escapes do not occur until one contestant is completely free of the other (Fig. 17).
6. To be sure that take downs do not occur until one wrestler has taken his opponent off his feet and has complete control over him (Fig. 18).
7. To see that a near fall does not occur until both shoulders are held continuously within two inches of the mat for two seconds. The points are not awarded until the defensive wrestler has escaped from the pinning combination (Fig. 19).
8. To see that a fall does not occur until both shoulders are held continuously to the mat for two seconds (Figs. 20, 21, 22).
9. To be alert to prevent injury where there is no side mat.
10. To be alert when there is a pinning combination along the edge of the mat.

11. To be in a proper position when one wrestler is about to pin the other.
12. To see if the top man is stalling and making no effort to pin.
13. To see if the bottom man plays the edge of the mat to keep out of trouble.
14. To see if the underneath man slides off the mat to keep from getting pinned.
15. To be sure the contestants do not leave the mat without permission.

Fig. 15.—Referee in the proper position at the edge of the mat.

Most of the difficult decisions are made at the edge of the mat. The official will have to decide whether the change of position was made before he went off the mat or after they left the mat. Many of these can be hairline decisions. Many of these difficult decisions are made when a fall is imminent and he will have to decide whether the wrestler went off the mat before a fall was secured or there was a near fall, or if there should be no points awarded.

In any case the referee should be in position to see their supporting points and the edge of the mat. This is very important in case there is a flurrie along the edge of the mat.

Making Decisions and Awarding Points: The referee must have a thorough background in wrestling if he hopes to make the correct decisions. This is particularly important when one wrestler has control over the other from a take down, or reverse, or when one has escaped to a neutral position.

Fig. 16.—Referee awarding two points for a reverse.

Fig. 17.—The referee awarding one point for escape.

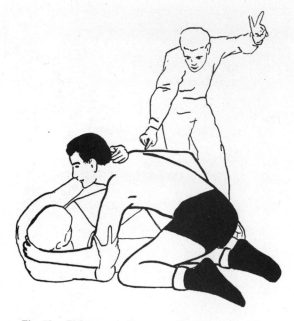

Fig. 18.—Referee awarding two points for a take down.

Fig. 19.—Referee awarding two points for a near fall.

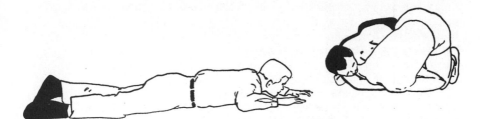

Fig. 20.—Referee in position to call a fall or near fall.

Fig. 21.—Referee has hand raised to call a fall when he has completed his silent count.

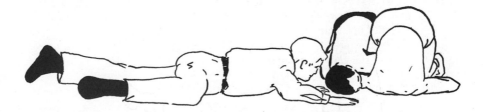

Fig. 22.—Referee has hit the mat with his hand to call a fall.

In scoring a take down, one wrestler must have taken his opponent to the mat from a standing position and have complete control over him down on the mat. As soon as the referee feels one wrestler has gained control over the other he shall award two points for a take town by pointing to the wrestler who has gained the advantage, at the same time holding his other hand high above his head with two fingers up indicating two points have been awarded. When these two points are awarded this signals to the time keeper who is keeping time advantage for this particular wrestler that he is to start his watch and keep it going until the official signals another change of position.

The reverse shall be called in the same manner as a take down. The underneath man must have reversed his position and gained complete control over his opponent. Not until then should the referee award two points for a reverse and it should be done in the same manner as for a take down.

If the man in the underneath position comes to his feet and gets completely free from his opponent he has earned an escape and shall be awarded one point. The referee shall award this point in the same manner as he did for a take down or reverse, except he holds up one finger.

Take downs, reverses, and escapes must be made on the mat proper. There will be many situations during the course of a wrestling match when one contestant has almost made a complete change of position, just as they go off the mat proper. In which case they must resume wrestling in the center of the mat as if no change has been made and no points are awarded.

Situations such as these will determine whether the official is capable. Many of these decisions will have to be hairline and the referee's action will determined whether he has developed qualities of calmness, reaction time, judgment, consistency, confidence, and a thorough knowledge of the rules.

Calling Falls and Near Falls: One of the hardest problems that a referee is confronted with during the course of a wrestling match is to determine falls and near falls. Often the contestants are so entangled that it is difficult for an official to take the proper position to see whether a wrestler is pinned. Many times it is almost impossible for a referee to see both shoulders because head, arms and elbows, or legs may block his view. The rules state that an opponent must hold the defensive man's shoulders in contact with the mat for continuous silent count of two seconds. It further states that the referee cannot start counting until he is in position to see that both shoulders are touching the mat. Oftentimes the offensive wrestler holds the defensive man's shoulders to the mat longer than two seconds simply because the official is not in position to start his count. It is imperative that the referee be alert and anticipate such situations before they arise.

In calling a fall the referee should be down on the mat in a position where he can see both shoulders touching the mat proper. Just as he starts his silent count he should raise one hand above his head. As the two-second count is made, he strikes the mat with the palm of his hand. This indicates that a fall has occurred and that the match is over.

A near fall occurs when the offensive wrestler has his opponent in a pinning combination and a fall is imminent. The defensive wrestler's shoulders must be held continuously within two inches of the mat for two seconds.   No near fall shall be awarded until the defensive wrestler has escaped this pinning situation.

The referee must be in the same position as for a fall and cannot start counting until he can see both shoulders are within two inches of the mat. When a near fall has occurred and the defensive wrestler has broken out of the pinning combination he shall call two points in the same manner as he did for take downs and reverses.

Awarding Points for Time Advantage: Time advantage begins when one contestant has brought the other to the mat or has reversed him and gained control of his opponent.   The time advantage watch does not start until the referee has awarded two points either for a take down or a reverse.   Time advantage continues until the defensive wrestler has reversed or escaped in which case the assistant time keeper continues until the referee has awarded his points for a reverse or an escape.   The referee must make sure that the timers have caught his signal.   If there is any uncertainty about the signal or awarding of points the match should be stopped immediately and the situation clarified.

Fig. 23.—Referee signals that wrestling is to stop.   He sounds his whistle.

The timers must understand the official time out signal.   Oftentimes the contestant goes off the mat and it will be necessary for the referee to call time out. Also, they must catch his signal to start wrestling.

In case of an injury the referee shall notify the head timer immediately as he must keep this time out period.   No contestant shall be allowed more than three minutes time out during the course of a wrestling match except for a nose bleed.

At the end of the bout the referee shall check with the timers to see if there are any points to be awarded for time advantage.   They shall subtract the difference of the accumulated time of the two contestants.   If one has accumulated less than one minute over the other there will be no points awarded for riding time.   If there is more than one minute but less than two minutes there shall be one point awarded for riding time and if there are two or more minutes of accumulated time difference between the two contestants there will be two points awarded.   At no time will more than two points be awarded for time advantage regardless of how many minutes one contestant has over the other.

Awarding the Match: In awarding the match at the end of the bout the referee should go through the following procedure:

1.   If the match is ended by a fall the referee shall have the two contestants shake hands and at the same time raise the left arm of the winner vertically (Fig. 24).

2.   Where the match is not terminated by a fall he will order the contestants to their corners to await a decision.

Fig. 24.—Awarding a decision or a fall.

3. He will then check with the scorer and timers to get the points scored during the match.
4. Once he has made his decision he shall call the contestants to the center of the mat.
5. They shall shake hands and at the same time the referee shall raise the left arm of the winner over his head vertically.
6. If the match turns out to be a draw he shall raise the left arms of both wrestlers vertically while they are shaking hands (Fig. 25).

Fig. 25.—Referee declaring a draw.

In Case of Injuries: When a contestant is injured the referee shall allow a maximum of three minutes rest. A wrestler has no limit to the number of rest periods he may have during the course of a wrestling match, just so the total time does not exceed three minutes. When the match starts after a rest period it shall start as if the contestants had gone out of bounds.

When the injury occurs the referee should notify the head timer that time is out because of an injury. The head timer has a watch which is set aside for this purpose which he should start immediately to keep time on this rest period.

The referee must decide immediately when the accident occurs whether it was accidental or was caused by an illegal hold. He will be in better position to render a decision if the injured contestant is unable to continue wrestling after the rest period.

If the injury was accidental they shall resume wrestling at the end of the rest period as if they went off the mat.   And if the injured contestant is unable to continue wrestling he shall forfeit to his opponent.   In this case his opponent shall receive the same number of points as if he had secured a fall.

If this injury was caused by an illegal hold and the injured contestant is able to continue wrestling after the rest period, he shall be awarded two points on the first penalty with no change of positions.   If the contestant cannot continue the match after the rest period because of an illegal hold the referee shall forfeit the match to him and he shall be awarded the same number of points toward team score as if he had won by a fall.

After the Match: There are certain general principles the referee should follow immediately after a wrestling meet, these are as follows;

1.   Any comments that spectators make after the meet should be ignored.
2.   He must never make any comments to the press or public concerning the match.
3.   The official should never ask the coach to comment on how he worked the meet.
4.   He must not make alibis or pass the buck.
5.   If the coach gets nasty, the official must keep silent.   But he should not work meets again for this type of a coach.
6.   The official should leave the scene of the contest immediately and go to the dressing room.
7.   If the official is called upon to rate the school officials and contestants, he should wait a few days for a cooling off period.

index